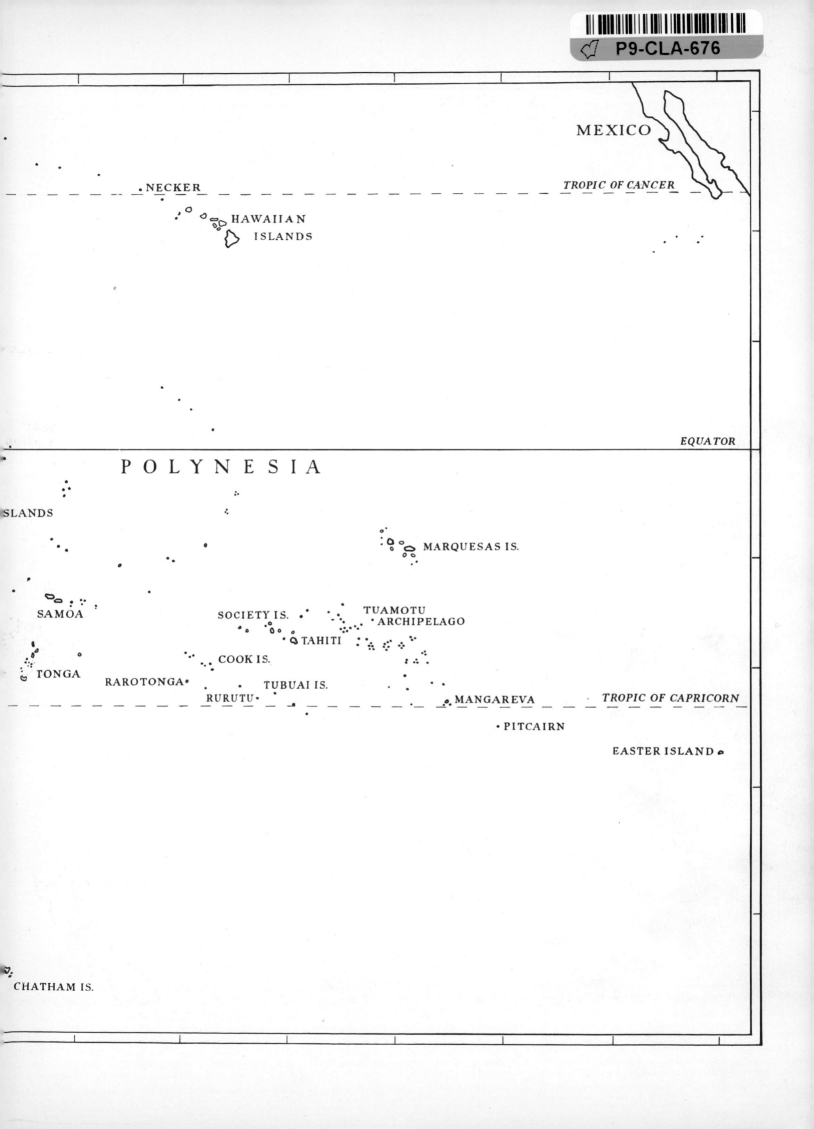

MEXICO

TROPIC OF CANCER

• NECKER

HAWAIIAN
ISLANDS

EQUATOR

P O L Y N E S I A

SLANDS

MARQUESAS IS.

SAMOA

SOCIETY IS.

TUAMOTU
ARCHIPELAGO

TAHITI

COOK IS.

TONGA

RAROTONGA

TUBUAI IS.

RURUTU

MANGAREVA

TROPIC OF CAPRICORN

• PITCAIRN

EASTER ISLAND

CHATHAM IS.

OCEANIC ART

OCEANIC ART

96 Photographs by

FRIEDRICH HEWICKER

Text by

HERBERT TISCHNER

PANTHEON BOOKS

TEXT PRINTED IN THE U. S. A.

GRAVURE PLATES PRINTED BY ETS BRAUN ET CIE, MULHOUSE, FRANCE

OCEANIC ART

"SOUTH SEAS": the expression was first coined by the Spanish conquistador Vasco Nuñez de Balboa when, on that fateful twenty-eighth of September, 1513, he and his small company of men, in their search for the legendary land of gold, gazed southwards from the low line of hills at Quarequa in what is now Panama, across an uninterrupted expanse of water stretching to the far horizon. From the time of Rousseau onwards these two words have, as it were unconsciously, conjured up in our minds a kind of earthly paradise, a far-off dream-world of blue seas and islands peopled by happier mortals than ourselves. Balboa christened it "Mar del Sur" and solemnly claimed it on behalf of the Spanish Crown.

Seven years later this vastest of the oceans of the world was traversed by the first white man, Fernão de Magalhães, a Portuguese in the service of the Spaniards, during one of the most daring voyages in history. It was a journey into the unknown, beset by perils, hunger, thirst and death. For four whole months the intrepid adventurers saw nothing, apart from two tiny uninhabited islets, but sky and water: by an extraordinary stroke of ill-fortune they steered a course which took them right between the many thousand islands. It was remarkable, too, that this often stormy ocean, visited as it is by devastating hurricanes, remained so calm during the whole of the voyage, that Magellan—to give him his more familiar name—called it the "Mar Pacífico", or Pacific Ocean. After 1,124 days at sea her few surviving hands sailed the *Victoria*, the only remaining ship of this little fleet—indeed, the first ship ever to circumnavigate the globe—into her home port of San Lúcar in Spain.

It was the Spaniards once again who—this time from Callao—set out on fresh voyages of discovery, obsessed by the lure of gold and the call of "Terra Australis", the mysterious, unknown Land of the South. In 1568 Álvaro de Mendaña came across the first large island group. Just as in America, so here in the South Seas, the Spaniards saw their phantasmagoria everywhere about them in the shape of the treasures of El Dorado and of Ophir, the Golden Land. So they named this Melanesian group "Islas de Salomón", under the mistaken impression that it was from here that King Hiram had fetched the gold for King Solomon's temple in Jerusalem. The second Mendaña expedition in 1595 also led to the discovery of an important archipelago, this time away in the east of the Pacific Ocean: the Marquesas. The magnificent natives, completely naked but with their entire bodies decoratively tattooed, were the first Polynesians to be encountered by Westerners; it was from their mouths that Europeans for the first time heard issue the melodic Polynesian tongue, so rich in vowel-sounds. However, the hopes of finding gold proved illusory, and so these discoveries lapsed into limbo for close upon 200 years, until Captain James Cook, with his three famous voyages, inaugurated the era of great discovery and scientific research in the South Seas.

By comparison with the huge expanse of the Pacific Ocean, which covers one-third of the surface of the globe, the 30,000-odd islands actually making up what we call Oceania are spread over a relatively small area, nearly all, with the exception of the double island of New Zealand, lying in the tropical zone. Following an old geographical division, the Oceanic island territory is split up also ethnologically into three main areas: Melanesia, Polynesia and Micronesia. These derive their names from the Greek, and mean respectively: "black island world", that part of south-west Oceania where in the big volcanic or ancient continental islands the dark-skinned natives live; "world of many islands", which embraces the vast triangular eastern zone, bounded in the north by Hawaii, in the south by New Zealand and in the east by Easter Island; finally, "world of little islands", consisting for the most part of countless little islets of coralline origin, the so-called atolls.

Ethnological research has shown that the South Sea Islands were settled as a result of several migrations from the West extending over long periods of time. The Melanesians were very early immigrants from south-east Asia. Much later, some three thousand years ago, the Polynesians arrived there, likewise from the Asian mainland via the Malay archipelago. The Micronesians are a mixed race of predominantly Polynesian strain. Furthermore, we still encounter what are the oldest racial elements in Melanesia: isolated remnants of pigmy stock and, above all in the interior of New Guinea, those stocky little, dark-skinned and—as their name implies—fuzzy-haired aborigines, the Papuans.

Melanesians, Polynesians and Micronesians, together with the Indonesians, are so closely related linguistically that they have all been grouped together under the name of "Austro-nesians" or "Malayo-Polynesians". They are unexcelled as ocean-faring folk and colonisers, for they systematically explored and settled more than half the surface of the globe—from Madagascar to Easter Island; indeed the Polynesians penetrated as far as Antarctica, and with their 130-foot-long double canoes undoubtedly reached the west coast of America. Their own tradition shows that the peak migration period for these "Vikings of the Sunrise" was from about A.D. 700 to 1200. Their highly developed art of navigation, though without benefit of compass, made the Polynesians the proud conquerors of this ocean world. They steered with almost unerring aim towards each and every desired island during journeys of many hundreds of miles. The voyages of the Melanesians, on the other hand, were confined almost entirely to the coasts and neighbouring islands.

Throughout Oceania, as in all other parts of the world, traditional culture has almost entirely disintegrated since the first contact with the white man was established. We should never lose sight of the fact that for this reason the original South Seas cultures, with the exception of the remoter parts of Melanesia, belong as much to the past as do the works of art to which they once gave rise.

The South Sea Islanders were a people without a written language, who in Polynesia could boast a remarkably live and long-established tradition. There were well-organised societies consisting of Neolithic tillers of the soil and fisherfolk, based partly on matrilineal, partly on patrilineal systems; in the Melanesian islands the social order found expression in chieftainship, age-class systems, secret societies and initiation ceremonies for young men, as well as in the closely allied usages associated with the mask.

The religious orientation of the Melanesians manifested itself in a belief in ghosts and witchcraft, and a deep-rooted ancestor-worship. Totemism, too, which exercised a direct and powerful influence upon social conditions, and of which traces only are still to be found in the remaining islands, attained its highest peak in Melanesia. The Melanesian cultures show particularly clearly to what degree the concepts deriving from ancestor-worship, initiation, secret societies, masks and totemism have influenced and determined virtually their entire representational art, or indeed provided the original impulse towards any kind of artistic creation whatsoever. Even things which at first sight strike us as commonplace and trivial, such as insignificant-looking figure-ornamentation or geometrical designs on weapons and utensils, are for the native more often than not no mere decorative accessories resulting from a desire to elaborate or from a delight in what is beautiful, but the most essential part of the object; where, that is to say, the ornament or symbol possesses magical properties, which alone determine the object's value and effectiveness.

The highest law the Melanesian knows is the law of sib. Only by bearing this in mind can we understand his way of life. An action which to us perhaps seems criminal he may regard as a moral obligation, above all if it is in the interests of his lineage. However, in this context his tribe is not confined to the living, but includes also the spirits of the dead, whose existence the Melanesian takes for granted. He believes they possess greater powers than the tribe's living members. Hence ancestor-worship is the focal-point of his religion. He knows that he owes to his ancestors not only his life on earth, but also his cultural amenities, his customs, rites and accomplishments, his utensils, weapons and means of subsistence—in short, the wherewithal with which to hold his own in life's battle. But, above all, the blessings of his ancestors bring a person good fortune and success in all his undertakings. Since, however, the powers of the departed spirits can also be of a harmful nature, the Melanesian has to guard against offending the ancestor-spirit, or incurring its displeasure through some act of thoughtlessness. The Melanesians are convinced that the world around them is filled with the ghosts of their ancestors, who continue to take part in all the happenings within the community and are ever on the watch to see that the customs and religious rites are observed in the traditional manner. Furthermore, they set great store by being shown due veneration, which must take the form of certain favourite sacrifices.

Thus, fear of vengeance from the spirits of the departed, and an anxiety to ensure that their help and beneficent power, the Mana, shall be forthcoming, determine the elementary conservatism and intense religiosity which everywhere prevails. The Melanesian word "Mana" has become a theological concept and denotes a magical power—"the exceptionally potent"—attaching to human beings, animals and things, which is at the root of all that is out-of-the-ordinary.

So that he should have visible evidence that the ancestor-spirit was always close at hand, the Melanesian prepared a dwelling-place for his soul. As during a man's lifetime, so after death, the skull was regarded as the location of the soul. Therefore, by means of remodelling and painting, the skull was made to resemble as closely as possible the features of the departed. The devotedly prepared skulls of the ancestors were kept in special places, frequently in the interior of the men's club houses, together with ritual objects such as sacred flutes, bullroarers, dance masks and drums.

A complete mummification of the entire body can hardly be effected in the tropics, yet the Melanesian does not always content himself with the ancestor's skull alone: frequently he fashions from all manner of plant fibres life-size, realistic figures, which he surmounts with the skull. Such statues of ancestor-chiefs used to stand in the men's club houses in south-west Malekula (New Hebrides). Sacrifices were made in their presence, food was placed before them—for the souls need sustenance also in the Beyond—and they were prayed to. At a later stage the actual skull was no longer used; the whole effigy was carved—usually in wood, occasionally using tree-fern pith and chalk—or hewn from stone. Thus, the cult of the skull led to the ancestor-statue, which later departed more and more from the original lifelike image, and in individual cultures and island-groups resulted from time to time in the development of specific styles.

In view of this, we can readily understand that the Melanesian would in certain circumstances wish to make the spirit of the dead assume a more realistic and active form. For this purpose he employs at initiation and funeral ceremonies various kinds of masks, which are also put to use on other occasions. When he dons a mask, the wearer loses his own identity: either he genuinely believes himself to be the ancestor-spirit, or at least the uninitiated—above all, the women and children—think he is.

Amongst the coastal dwellers of the Gazelle Peninsula of New Britain the original pattern of this type of mask persisted well into our own times. It consisted of the shaped and painted facial portion with the lower jaw of the actual ancestral skull, and was held in front of the face of the wearer by means of a cross-piece tied to the back which he gripped between his teeth.

The noticeably wide range of grotesque Melanesian masks might give the impression that in this field the designer was permitted an exceptional degree of freedom. In point of fact, however, the amount of latitude allowed in the matter of individual variations is very small, and conformity with traditional precepts is as strictly observed as in every other branch of artistic creation. The mask-maker adheres in the main to the accepted forms, and individual variations are to be explained by the multiplicity of Melanesian areas of civilisation, islands and tribes.

The mask-dances are for the most part performed at certain specified times—preferably on moonlit nights or by the flickering light of torches—and there is something gruesomely fascinating and sinister about their animated rigidity. The men's secret societies, which are intimately concerned with the mask and its functions, see to it that the secret of these dances is kept. With solemn ceremonial, often accompanied by exacting tests and the threat of severe punishment, the novices to the secret society are bound to absolute secrecy. Masks are also worn by those who, as representatives of the ancestors, come to pluck from the bosom of their families and their accustomed way of life the young men who are to join the ritual community. The nature of the ensuing ceremonies would indicate that the novice is regarded as having died, in order that he may begin a new life as a person reborn. This process is often implied by bestowing upon the young man a new name, or symbolically by having him devoured by a monster made for this purpose out of plaited fibres or bark. This motive is also encountered in Australia, Africa and north-west America.

Male societies and the mask are characteristic of large areas of Melanesia, whereas they are virtually non-existent in Micronesia and Polynesia. But they do not necessarily always appear in conjunction. The Duk-Duk secret society of Duke of York Island and the neighbouring Gazelle Peninsula of New Britain achieved a certain notoriety, not least by virtue of the remarkable tall, pointed hat-masks that their members used. In olden times the Duk-Duk had its religious, judicial and social functions, and the natives found in its rigid organisation a firm prop. However, a progressive deterioration set in: in place of the mystery of death and regeneration the initiates were actuated by egoistical, material motives, and these manifested themselves in terror and oppression towards the remainder of the population.

No other Oceanic secret society so profoundly influenced the community and played so vital a part in the life and thought of the islanders, as the powerful Suque of the New Hebrides and Banks Islands. The Suque, which probably resulted from the merging of an old-established ancestor-cult with a more recent religion, can best be described as a pig-sacrificing cult. Every able-bodied male was drafted into the Suque system, which even determined the social order. The place of the chiefs who are customary in Melanesia was taken by the highest-ranking members of the secret society, and the social standing of all the other men corresponded to their rank within the Suque. The most significant aspect of this all-powerful society, however, concerned the individual's relationship to the Beyond, for it laid down as a basic principle that each man shall enjoy the benefits of the Suque even after death, in that he assumed in the world of the spirits the same rank that he had held in the world of the living. Every member was concerned to advance his social status as far as possible in this world already, and, correspondingly, his Suque rank. This, according to the rules of the society, could be achieved only through a succession of sacrifices over a period of time, sacrifices entailing certain types of pigs—namely, boars with tusks, whose growth was artificially cultivated to form a ring. The value of these carefully tended sacrificial beasts rose enormously as their age increased, and their tusks came to full development. The number of pigs required for a man to attain to the highest Suque rank could be as many as a hundred. Few only could rise to this. The number of secret society grades ranged on the islands from four to sixteen.

Men of the highest rank possessed the most Mana, since they were in spiritual communion with departed souls of like status; they were at once headmen and priests, enjoyed the esteem accorded to chieftains and were assured the happiest of fates in the Beyond. To join the Suque and to devote oneself to carrying out plenty of sacrifices was consequently a matter of religious obligation as well as of self-preservation.

Every native was able to recognise a man's Suque rank by the style in which his body was tattooed, and by certain ornaments and articles of clothing he wore. In addition, special statues used to be set up in the vicinity of the houses or in the bush: these figures, several yards high, were carved in wood or from the pith of the tree-fern, and indicated their owners' status. Serving a similar purpose were posts of a decorative nature on which several faces were carved, intended to convey that the owner united within himself the Mana of more than one person or ancestor-spirit; sometimes also sculptures with markedly stylised representations of the lower jaws of all the pigs sacrificed by him.

In the houses of the men's societies of south-west Malekula, which were similarly ornamented with figure carvings and—rather less frequently—with magical paintings, stood the aforementioned genuine skull statues of deceased chiefs, that is, of the most exalted members of the Suque; these, by virtue of their powerful Manas, it was considered desirable to try to maintain in their privileged status and make objects of worship. Such ancestor figures constituted an indissoluble link between the living and the spirit world.

The Suque is not found in the southern islands of the New Hebrides, nor are there traces of any kind of artistic creation worthy of the name.

Nowadays the Suque has practically disappeared, and life for the "honest heathens" has thereby been robbed of all meaning.

The natives of New Ireland and of a few of the smaller outlying islands use the term "Málanggan" to denote their funeral rites and the dances associated therewith, as well as the masks and numerous other carved objects used in this connection. In his *Geschichte der Kunst*

Karl Woermann writes of these: "Anyone who has ever seen them, is thereafter haunted as by a feverish dream." Indeed these remarkable carvings, with their fantastic intensity of expression, are the strangest things to be met with in the whole range of primitive art, and stand out even among all other types of Oceanic sculpture. The richness and variety of these painted masks, with their bewildering themes, of the ancestor figures and other ritual objects pertaining to this island of the Bismarck Archipelago is without parallel. As they appear to be unlike and unassociated with any other style, the "Málanggan style" has long since become an accepted ethnological term.

Celebrations in commemoration of the dead used to take place annually from the end of May until the beginning of July, and required months of preparation. In the first place the Málanggans had to be prepared, a task that—apart from a few types of mask—had to be carried out by special carving experts in the utmost secrecy in closely fenced-in places from which women and children were excluded. Certain sculptures and wood-reliefs in openwork style, frequently of huge dimensions, were kept altogether out of sight of the women, others were exhibited to the people at the beginning of the festivities and dancing by way of a great surprise, to the sound of singing and the beating of wooden drums. Such Málanggans as portrayed specific departed spirits, were greeted by those present with loud lamentations and cries of the dead man's name. Every Málanggan had its own story, to which the carvings and other ornamentation, in the shape of snakes, sharks and the like, alluded; totemic significance attached exclusively to representations of birds. Many Málanggans were purely decorative. With the exception of the Uli figures—that is, impersonal statues of chiefs around which a considerable part of the Málanggan festivities centred, and which were carefully preserved in special houses—all the carvings were burned or otherwise destroyed at the close of the festival period.

In contrast to Melanesia, a clearly defined aristocracy and a social order are to be found in Polynesia and Micronesia. In the Polynesian organisation of society there are even signs of the beginnings of a State structure. Micronesia evolved the hero-cult, which in Polynesia developed into the worship of deities.

All Polynesians were positively obsessed by the social scale. A man's status was determined solely by that of his parents, coupled with seniority by birth. In matrilineally orientated communities the child of a woman of royal blood and a commoner was accorded superior status to the offspring of a king and a woman of the people. Though the possibility may have existed for an individual to elevate himself by means of certain ceremonies on the Marae, the place of ritual, and through the sacrifice of the first-born, the whole Polynesian system of rank or status was based on the religious foundation of ancestor-worship, in that the Mana of all the ancestors was transmitted together with the rank. It is due to this traditional belief and custom that the Polynesians place such overwhelming importance upon their tribal and family genealogy; with this genealogy, extending back some eighty generations, of which the earliest must have merged into myth, every single individual was intimately acquainted through oral transmission; there were even schools in some parts for imparting such knowledge.

Although in parts of Polynesia the worship of deities would seem at first sight to have put ancestor-worship in the shade, it was nevertheless the latter which provided the developing social organisation with its underlying religious impetus, and was definitely closer to the native's heart than were his gods. This is particularly noticeable in the east, in the Marquesas and on Easter Island, where ancestor-worship found its artistic expression among other things in the monumental stone statues of the burial- and ritual-places, as well as in the truly remarkable male skeleton figures carved from wood. In Tahiti and the Cook Islands ancestor-worship was intermingled with the cult of those deities whose temples served as burial-places.

The Polynesian idols were by no means necessarily anthropomorphic; they sometimes consisted of quite other things, such as pieces of wood enclosed in plaited work and adorned with red and yellow feathers symbolising the god, idols resembling paddles or spears, a common stone, a conchshell trumpet and the like. It is significant, in this connection, that such outstanding Polynesian carvers as the Maoris never produced images of their great gods. All their figure-sculptures represent ancestors or heroes. They depicted their gods solely in the form of stick-shaped objects with symbols characteristic of the individual deities. And even in cases where actual images of gods were produced, these were not regarded as embodiments of the deities in question, but solely as objects of which the latter could take possession as and when they wished. In the little central Polynesian atoll of Tongareva, during the ritual feasts the gods had to content themselves with images made from plaited coco-nut leaves as temporary dwelling-places, which received no further attention once the ceremonies had ended. On the other hand it must be remembered that when, say in Tahiti, an idol fell to the ground outside the Marae, the spot affected became so taboo, that special ceremonies were necessary to make it accessible to the people again.

It is a curious fact that in Polynesia the art of carving reached its peak only in the outermost islands of the north, south and east; with very few exceptions, it made no headway in western Polynesia.

Among the numerous gods, demi-gods and deified ancestors, relatively few were accorded genuine veneration by the Polynesians. These included the creator-god and god of the ocean Tangaroa, and the three great gods Tane (Kane), Ku (Tu) and Rongo, who, though they are everywhere encountered from Hawaii to New Zealand, tended to possess varying attributes in the different island groups. Thus, Tane is the god of the forest, protector of artisans, above all the boat-builder, god of the heavens and of the light; Rongo, as the god of agriculture and of peace, is the mildest of the three, abhorring bloody sacrifices; Ku, the terrible god of war, by contrast, had countless victims—mainly enemy captives—sacrificed to him in the Hawaii of long ago.

A colourful web of myths has been spun around the Polynesian hero Maui. Men owe to him a number of useful discoveries and amenities, of which the foremost is fire. According to folk-lore, too, Maui fished several Polynesian islands out of the sea, amongst them Tahiti, Tongareva and the North Island of New Zealand, and to this day the Maori refer to the last-named as "the fish of Maui". Tradition frequently causes Maui to be merged with the demi-god Tiki, who appears sometimes as a god, at other times as the first man. It is after him that the Polynesian wooden and stone images of gods and the precious jade-amulet breast adornments of the Maori women of New Zealand are named "Tiki" and "Hei-Tiki", respectively. These ornaments are supposed by some to depict Tiki as an embryo, presumably because the Maui saga has it that Maui-Tiki-Tiki was born in embryo form and was thrown into the sea, though he was subsequently rescued by the ocean gods.

When we said that all the Oceanic peoples belonged to the Neolithic level of culture, we meant that until their contact with European civilisation every type of metal was unknown to them. They had to rely, therefore, for their raw materials and tools, on the other natural resources of their environment, such as wood, stone, clay, bones, teeth, shells and turtle shell. Despite the extremely difficult and tedious process of fashioning with stone and bone implements, with shark's-teeth and ray-skin rasps, the early natives for the most part used the hardest of woods for their carvings. But it was this very laboriousness that encouraged a conscientious and devoted attitude on the artist's part towards his work. With the introduction of iron knives and axes a deterioration in representational art soon set in. A second circumstance still further hastened this transition: since the creative art of the Oceanic peoples is practically always an expression of powerful religious emotions, the uprooting of the ancient beliefs inevitably resulted in the ruin of their art, for it lost its spiritual impulse. What began as a serious, consecrated task became a casual and meaningless way of passing the time, or even a money-making activity.

Traditions pertaining to the origin of Oceanic art repeatedly point to a god or a culture-bearer; for this reason the artists—the Tohunga, Tuhuna, Tufuna, Kahuna or whatever name they went by in the different Polynesian island groups and dialects—were among the most highly respected persons, being often at the same time tribal priests—that is, intermediaries between the people and the supernatural powers. Nothing illustrates better the status of the Tohunga in the tribal community than the fact that this almost untranslatable word is a collec-tive term meaning both artist—that is, in the first place, sculptor and tattooing expert—and medicine-man, house- and boat-builder, teacher in every sphere of knowledge and, not least, priest. All these and more callings—arts in the widest sense of the word—which could quite well be incorporated in a single person, counted as sacred, and every deviation from tradition was regarded as a bad omen. This notwithstanding, the works of art of the South Seas bear unmistakable signs of individual achievement and a creative personality. The work of all these "masters of ritual practices" was so sacred that it was initiated with invocations to the gods and

13

with ritual chanting. In Hawaii, once upon a time, a human sacrifice accompanied the carving of a god's likeness.

If we survey the works of art of the Oceanic peoples, it becomes clear that all of them, from the smallest ornament to the most monumental statue, are the result of limitless devotion and care; where they derive from ancient times, moreover, they manifest an unerring sense of form and a no less remarkable degree of aesthetic achievement. All this was the work of men whom the white man, in his arrogance, was pleased to call "savages", but who in truth possessed a culture many thousands of years old. There is a tendency, too, to picture the so-called primitive races, in particular the Melanesians among the peoples of the South Seas, as pitiful creatures, living in a perpetual state of superstitious dread. Yet one must—to use Felix Speiser's words —"ask oneself whether in such circumstances so rich, often indeed excessively rich, an art could well have come into existence, and one must also bear in mind that wherever such delight in the beauty of form and colour is evinced, the spirit cannot be living entirely in the shadows, but must know also joy".

The mental outlook and approach to life of the three large regions of Oceania are reflected in their art, though less pronouncedly so in the case of Micronesia. Over and above that, however, each island group, sometimes each individual island of an archipelago, and indeed on the larger islands, each separate tribe has developed its own individual style; this shows so small a range of variation—that is to say, is generally so characteristic—that it enables the expert to identify with certainty the origin of any work of art, or, for that matter, any ethnographic object. In the South Seas all art conforms to type. Even the still very undeveloped and naturalistic figural representations of the oldest culture-strata exhibit sufficient common criteria to enable us to classify them according to their origin, and group them together to form the so-called Primary style.

The correspondences in the outward form which constitute what we term style, though at first glance presenting a variegated mosaic, are found upon closer examination to exhibit a marked degree of conformity. Thus, Felix Speiser has been able not only to establish a series of clearly differentiated styles, but also to classify them genetically and chronologically, and to link some of them with specific waves of culture or migrations, which extend as far as India.

Speiser's theories concerning the art styles of Oceania may be briefly summarised as follows:

The chief characteristic of the "Primary style" is that it has not yet found a clear-cut form, and so is not yet strictly speaking a true style; "it can reappear at the lower artistic level of every culture".

The "Curvilinear" must be regarded as the first properly developed style. It is encountered in the very old Papuan strain of New Guinea, in particular on the Sepik River, around the Gulf of Papua and in the Bismarck Archipelago among the Baining, ostensibly the oldest inhabitants of New Britain. It still pervades the Trobriand Islands, while the remainder of Melanesia is noticeably little influenced by it and, so far as Polynesia is concerned, it has extended only to New Zealand. "By no means every object that shows curves"—which, theoretically, may occur anywhere—"should," says Speiser, "be treated as belonging to the Curvilinear style, but only such works as suggest that the straight line is positively repugnant to their maker, that his natural mode of artistic expression is the curve, which he everywhere seeks. . . ." We can distinguish several distinct variations in the Curvilinear style, and it is to be presumed that in the various territories where it occurs it derives from "the natural inclination of all Papuans to use this form". In places it has become merged with later styles.

The "Beak style", too, so named because of the beak-like extension of the nose as far as the navel or the genitalia, "likewise takes the curve as its basis and has little use for the straight line". A further characteristic of its largely anthropomorphic carvings is the slant of the eyes. This style is a feature of the northern coast of New Guinea on either side of the Sepik Estuary, and can be traced—though here it is less readily recognisable—eastwards across the western Solomon Islands and the New Hebrides as far as New Caledonia. The origins of the Beak style have not yet been definitely ascertained; but Speiser is inclined to relate it to the revered Indian god of wisdom, the elephant-shaped Ganesha, suggesting that the remarkable elongated nose of the Beak style may possibly derive from the elephant's trunk. Hindu elements, he maintains, could have caused the Ganesha cult to spread along the north-east coast of New Guinea, where it is conceivable that the here "unknown elephant may have undergone a transformation into something bird-like under the influence of the Curvilinear style".

Another more recent style is the "Korwar style", so named after the figured wooden receptacles for ancestor skulls of north-west New Guinea. Among its characteristics are the cubic shape of the head with its very broad mouth near the horizontally sliced-off chin, and the squatting position of the figure, which often holds a second, smaller one in front of it. The fact that it is to be found mainly in the extreme north-west of New Guinea, that the figures are frequently shown with the Malayan pointed hat and with the straight hair which is equally foreign to the Melanesians, points to the Korwar style also having originated in the west, for it is much in evidence in Indonesia as far as Sumatra and Nias. Farther east, the Korwar style is found predominantly in the Solomon Islands, and finally crops up again in eastern Polynesia —in the Marquesas, Easter Island and, less surely, in New Zealand. It seems possible to trace back the Korwar style to the Khmer art of Indo-China; that is—as in the case of the Beak style—to an Asiatic culture.

A typically Melanesian style is that which is to be found at its purest and most expressive in the carvings of Tami Island and along the east coast of Astrolabe Bay as far as Huon Gulf. Ethnologically it is known as the "Tami style", and is recognisable, in contrast to the Korwar style, primarily by the prismatic shape of the head, which is nearly always set noticeably low between the shoulders. A favourite form of ornamentation are the grooves in which triangles are engraved. These figures are often provided with looped spirals carved from the wood block, by which they are hung. A favourite motif of this style is one depicting a snake or a crocodile devouring a human being.

The "Málanggan style", already referred to, is entirely restricted to the small area of northern New Ireland and its outlying islands. Technically accomplished, it is instinct with "a striving for genuine plasticity, in which the interest is not centred on one main aspect as in other Melanesian figures; instead, many Málanggan figures are quite obviously intended to be viewed from any angle". The almost overwhelming abundance of motifs and the richness and intricacy of the openwork carving "is elsewhere virtually confined to Hindu art, and one may seriously wonder whether Málanggan art does not represent an offshoot of Indian sculpture, and not a very old one at that". Even the manifold representations of the bird with the snake would seem to find their parallels in the divine Indian Garuda bird and the Naga serpent.

These art styles, the definition of which Speiser has based upon extensive research and much expert knowledge, may perhaps need some checking and supplementing in matters of detail, but he has almost certainly arrived at general principles which should serve as a guide for future work in this field.

BIBLIOGRAPHY

1. On the Art of the South Seas

Adam, L. *Primitive Art*. London, 1949.

Cahiers D'Arts. *Fascicule consacré à l'art des Océaniens*. No. 2-3. Paris, 1929.

Chauvet, St. *Art de la Nouvelle Guinée*. Paris, 1930.

Chauvet, St. *L'Ile de Pâques et ses mystères*. Paris, 1935.

Firth, R. *Art and Life in New Guinea*. London-New York, 1936.

Haddon, A. C. *The Decorative Art of British New Guinea*. London, 1894.

Hamilton, A. *Maori Art. The Art Workmanship of the Maori Race in New Zealand*. Dunedin, 1896.

Handy, W. C. *L'Art des Iles Marquises*. Paris, 1938.

Krämer, A. *Die Málanggane von Tombára*. Munich, 1925.

Kühn, H. *Die Bedeutung der prähistorischen und ethnographischen Kunst für die Kunstgeschichte*. (Ipek, vol. 1, 1925.)

L'Art Océanien. Collection. Le Musée vivant. No. 38. Paris, 1951.

Leenhardt, M. *Arts de l'Océanie*. Paris, 1947. (London, 1950.)

Linton, R./Wingert, P. S. *Arts of the South Seas*. New York, 1946.

Luquet, G. H. *L'Art Néo-Calédonien*. Paris, 1926.

Luquiens, H. M. *Hawaiian Art*. Honolulu, 1931.

Nevermann, H. *Südseekunst*. Berlin, 1933.

Oldman, W. O. *The Oldman Collection of Polynesian Artifacts*. New Plymouth, 1943.

Oldman, W. O. *Skilled Handwork of the Maori. Being the Oldman Collection of Maori Artifacts*. Wellington, N.Z., 1946.

Speiser, F. *Kunststile in der Südsee*. Basle, 1941. (Führer durch das Museum für Völkerkunde Basel.)

Speiser, F. *Über Kunststile in Melanesien*. (Zeitschrift für Ethnologie, vol. 68, 1936.)

Stolpe, H. *Entwicklungserscheinungen in der Ornamentik der Naturvölker*. (Mitteilungen der Anthroposophischen Gesellschaft Wien, vol. 22, 1892.)

Steinen, K. v. d. *Die Marquesaner und ihre Kunst*. 3 vols. Berlin, 1925-28.

Vatter, E. *Religiöse Plastik der Naturvölker*. Frankfurt a.M., 1926.

Sydow, E. v. *Die Kunst der Naturvölker und der Vorzeit*. (Propyläen-Kunstgeschichte.) Berlin, 1923.

Sydow, E. v. *Kunst und Religion der Naturvölker*. Oldenburg, 1926.

Wingert, P. S. *Arts of the South Pacific Islands*. London, 1953.

2. On the Ethnography of the South Seas

Andersen, J. C. *Myths and Legends of the Polynesians*. London, 1928.

Andersen, J. C. *The Maori Tohunga and his Spirit World*. New Plymouth, 1948.

Archey, G. *South Sea Folk: Handbook of Maori and Oceanic Ethnology*. Auckland, 1937.

Beckwith, M. *Hawaiian Mythology*. New Haven, 1940.

Best, E. *The Maori*. 2 vols. Wellington, N.Z., 1924.

Behrmann, W. *Im Stromgebiet des Sepik*. Berlin, 1922.

Brown, J. M. *Melanesians and Polynesians*. London, 1910.

Buck, P. H. (Te Rangi Hiroa.) *Vikings of the Sunrise*. New York, 1938.

Bühler, A. *Neuirland und Nachbarinseln*. Basle, 1948. (Führer durch das Museum für Völker-kunde Basel.)

Codrington, R. H. *The Melanesians. Studies in their Anthropology and Folk-lore*. Oxford, 1891.

Dittmer, W. *Te Tohunga. Alte Sagen aus Maoriland*. Hamburg, o.J.

Edge-Partington, J./Heape, Ch. *An Album of the Weapons, Tools, Ornaments, Articles of Dress etc. of the Natives of the Pacific Islands*. 3 vols. Manchester, 1890-98.

Finsch, O. *Südseearbeiten*. Hamburg, 1914.

Firth, R. *Primitive Polynesian Economy*. London, 1939.

Fox, C. E. *The Threshold of the Pacific. An Account of the Social Organisation, Magic and Religion of the People of San Cristoval in the Solomon Islands*. London, 1924.

Friederici, G. *Malaio-Polynesische Wanderungen*. Leipzig, 1914.

Handy, E. S. C. *Polynesian Religion*. Honolulu, 1927.

Henry, T. *Ancient Tahiti*. Honolulu, 1928.

Hiroa, Te Rangi. *Arts and Crafts of the Cook Islands*. Honolulu, 1944.

Hiroa, Te Rangi. *An Introduction to Polynesian Anthroplogy*. Honolulu, 1945.

Hiroa, Te Rangi. *The Coming of the Maori*. Wellington, N.Z., 1950.

Hogbin, H. Ian. *Peoples of the Southwest Pacific*. New York, 1945.

Hurley, Fr. *Pearls and Savages. Adventures in the Air, on Land and Sea in New Guinea*. New York-London, 1924.

Krämer, A. *Die Samoa-Inseln*. 2 vols. Stuttgart, 1903.

Krämer, A. *Hawaii. Ostmikronesien und Samoa*. Stuttgart, 1906.

Krämer, A. *Palau*. 5 vols. (Ergebnisse der Südsee-Expedition 1908-10.) Hamburg, 1919-26.

Krämer-Bannow, E. *Bei kunstsinnigen Kannibalen der Südsee*. Berlin, 1916.

Landtman, G. *The Kiwai Papuans of British New Guinea*. London, 1927.

Laval, H. *Mangareva. L'Histoire ancienne d'un Peuple Polynésien*. Braine-le Comte, 1938.

Layard, J. *Stone Men of Malekula*. London, 1942.

Lehmann, F. R. *Mana. Der Begriff des "Außerordentlich Wirkungsvollen" bei Südseevölkern*. Leipzig, 1922.

Lehmann, F. R. *Die polynesischen Tabusitten*. Leipzig, 1930.

Lewis, A. B. *The Melanesians. People of the South Pacific*. Chicago, 1951.

Le Roux, C. C. F. M. *De Bergpapoea's van Nieuw Guinea en hun Woongebied*. 2 vols. and atlas. Leiden, 1950.

Linton, R. *Ethnology of Polynesia and Micronesia*. Chicago, 1926.

Malinowski, B. *Argonauts of the West Pacific*. London, 1922.

Malo, D. *Hawaiian Antiquities*. Honolulu, 1951.

Métraux, A. *Ethnology of Easter Island*. Honolulu, 1940.

Mülhmann, W. E. *Staatsbildung und Amphiktyonien in Polynesien*. Stuttgart, 1938.

Müller-Wismar, W. *Yap*. 2 vols. (Ergebnisse der Südsee-Expedition 1908-10.) Hamburg, 1917-18.

Neuhauss, R. *Deutsch-Neuguinea*. 3 vols. Berlin, 1911.

Nevermann, H. *Admiralitäts-Inseln*. (Ergebnisse der Südsee-Expedition 1908-10.) Hamburg, 1934.

Nevermann, H. *Masken und Geheimbünde in Melanesien*. Berlin, 1933.

Nevermann, H. *Götter der Südsee*. Stuttgart, 1947.

Oldman, W. O. *The Oldman Collection of Polynesian Artifacts.* New Plymouth, 1943.

Oldman, W. O. *Skilled Handwork of the Maori. Being the Oldman Collection of Maori Artifacts.* Wellington, N.Z., 1946.

Parkinson, R. *Dreißig Jahre in der Südsee.* Stuttgart, 1907.

Peekel, G. *Religion und Zauberei auf dem mittleren Neu-Mecklenburg.* Münster, i.W., 1910.

Reche, O. *Der Kaiserin-Augusta-Fluß.* (Ergebnisse der Südsee-Expedition 1908-10.) Hamburg, 1913.

Reischeck, A. *Sterbende Welt, Zwölf Jahre Forscherleben auf Neuseeland.* Leipzig, 1924.

Reports of the Cambridge Anthropological Expedition to Torres-Straits. 6 vols. Cambridge, 1901-35.

Riesenfeld, A. *The Megalithic Culture of Melanesia.* Leiden, 1950.

Rivers, W. H. R. *History of Melanesian Society.* 2 vols. Cambridge, 1914.

Sarasin, F. *Neu-Caledonien und die Loyalty-Inseln.* Basle, 1917.

Sarasin, F. *Ethnologie der Neu-Caledonier und Loyalty-Insulaner.* München, 1929.

Schulze-Maizier, F. *Die Osterinsel.* Leipzig, o.J.

Speiser, F. *Südsee, Urwald, Kannibalen. Reisen in den Neuen-Hebriden und Sta-Crus-Inseln.* Stuttgart, 1924.

Speiser, F. *Ethnographische Materialien aus den Neuen-Hebriden und Banks-Inseln.* Berlin, 1923.

Speiser, F. *Über Initiationen in Australien und Neuguinea.* (Verhandlungen der Naturforsch. Ges. Basel, vol. 40, Basle, 1929.)

Seligmann, C. G. *The Melanesians of British New Guinea.* Cambridge, 1910.

Vicedom, F. G./Tischner. H. *Die Mbowamb. Die Kultur der Hagenbergstämme im östlichen Zentral-Neuguinea.* 3 vols. Hamburg, 1943-48.

Williams, F. E. *Orokaiva Society.* Oxford, 1928.

Williams, F. E. *Orokaiva Magic.* Oxford, 1930.

Wirz, P. *Die Marindanim von Holländisch-Süd-Neu-Guinea.* 2 vols. Hamburg, 1922-25.

3. On the History of Discovery in the South Seas

Beaglehole, J. C. *The Exploration of the Pacific.* London, 1934.

Bougainville, L. A. de. *Voyage autour du Monde par la Frégate du Roi la Boudeuse et la flute L'Etoile.* Paris, 1771.

Brosses, Ch. de. *Histoire des Navigations aux Terres Australes.* 2 vols. Paris, 1756.

Burney, J. *A chronological History of the Discoveries in the South Sea or Pacific Ocean.* 5 vols. London, 1805-17.

Chamisso, A. v. *Reise um die Welt mit der Romanzoffischen Entdeckungs-Expedition in den Jahren 1815-18.* Leipzig, 1836.

Cook, J. *A Voyage towards the South Pole and round the World.* 2 vols. London, 1777.

Dalrymple, A. *An historical Collection of the several Voyages and Discoveries in the South Pacific Ocean.* 2 vols. London, 1770.

Forster, G. *Johann Reinhold Forsters Reise um die Welt während den Jahren 1772-75.* 2 vols. Berlin, 1778.

Hawkesworth, J. *An Account of the Voyages . . . for making Discoveries in the Southern Hemisphere . . .* (Byron, Wallis, Carteret, Cook). 3 vols. London, 1773.

Hiroa, Te Rangi. *Explorers of the Pacific.* Honolulu, 1953.

Kotzebue, O. v. *Entdeckungsreise in die Süd-See und nach der Bering-Strasse.* 3 vols. Weimar, 1821.

Krusenstern, A. J. v. *Reise um die Welt in den Jahren 1803, 1804, 1805 und 1806—auf den Schiffen Nadeshda und Newa.* 3 vols. St. Petersburg, 1810.

Langsdorff, G. H. v. *Bemerkungen auf einer Reise um die Welt in den Jahren 1803 bis 1807.* 2 vols. Frankfurt a.M., 1812.

La Pérouse, J. F. G. de. *Voyage de la Pérouse autour du Monde . . . redigé par M. L. A. Milet-Mureau.* 4 vols. and atlas. Paris, 1797.

Le Maire, J./Schouton, W. C. *De Ontdekkingsreis van Jacob le Maire en William Cornelisz. Schouten in de Jaren 1615-1617. Uitg. door W. A. Engelbrecht en P. J. van Herwerden.* 2 vols. 's-Gravenhage, 1945.

Lorscheid, J. *Die von Callao ausgegangenen Entdeckungsfahrten der Spanier in die Südsee.* Rheydt, 1903.

Mendaña, Alvaro de. *The Discovery of the Solomon Islands by Alvaro de Mendaña in 1568.* Ed. by Lord Amherst of Hackney and Basil Thomson. 2 vols. London, 1901.

Tasman, A. J. *Abel Janszoon Tasman's Journal of his Discovery of Van Diemens Land and New Zealand in 1642 . . . Facsimiles of the original Manuscript . . . with English translation . . .* by J. E. Heeres. Amsterdam, 1898.

NOTES

1 RITUAL PAINTING FROM A CEREMONIAL HOUSE (usually known as a CLUB HOUSE).
Melanesia (Village of Kambrambo, Lower Sepik River, New Guinea).
The interior walls of ceremonial houses are covered with paintings like this one.
Sago-palm bark painted black, red and white.
Height, 100 cm. (39⅜ in.).
Basle Museum (V b. 9409).

2 SUSPENSION HOOK.
Melanesia (Sepik River, New Guinea).
Hooks such as this one, often beautifully carved, are used inside the houses for hanging up net bags and other household articles.
Heavy, dark wood; face painted black, white and red; traces of red colouring on the chest; mother-of-pearl eyes; ears decorated with tufts of grass.
Height, 96 cm. (37¾ in.).
Berne Museum (Pap. 1114).

3 RITUAL STOOL.
Melanesia (Sepik River, New Guinea).
So-called ritual stools, usually carved in human shape —possibly to represent an ancestor or some spirit— stand in the ceremonial houses of villages along the Sepik River. In formal assemblies, when affairs of general importance are discussed, the orators touch them to emphasise the points of their speech.
Wood, painted pink; crescent-shaped breast ornament, frontal disk and heart-shaped carving of the face in white. Eyes made of the large white bases of conus shells and surrounded by black and white drop-shaped pattern. Tufts of human hair; suggestion of scars round the navel (the natives have scars cut on their bodies during initiation ceremonies). Supports at the back in the shape of fishes with bent heads.
Height, 162 cm. (63¾ in.).
Berne Museum (Pap. 1157).

4 SUSPENSION HOOK.
Melanesia (Middle Sepik River, New Guinea).
See note for plate 2.
The carved lines on chest, arms and particularly round the navel are a realistic rendering of the scars which the natives cut on the young men during initiation ceremonies. The fringed loin-cloth is of the kind worn by the men of this region.

Wood, painted pink and white. Beard of real human hair.
Height, 139 cm. (54¾ in.).
Neuchâtel Museum (V. 881).

5 LARGE FIGURE.
Melanesia (Lower Sepik River, New Guinea).
Probably the statue of an ancestor or spirit.
Very light, pale wood, painted black, white and red.
Height, 147 cm. (57⅞ in.).
Bremen Museum (D. 4130).

6 CANOE WAR SHIELD.
Melanesia (Middle Sepik River, New Guinea).
These shields accompanied the Sepik warriors on their expeditions and were put up behind the bows—mostly carved in the shape of a crocodile—of their great dug-out canoes (which, on the Sepik River, had no outrigger).
Sago-palm bark over wicker frame, painted black and white; mouth and forehead of attached wooden mask painted pink. Eyes of white conus-shell bases, surrounded by black cassowary feathers. Beard of trimmed bunches of feathers from the same bird.
Width, 85 cm. (33½ in.).
Berne Museum (Pap. 1149).

7 RITUAL STOOL.
Melanesia (Sepik River, New Guinea).
See note for plate 3.
Wood, plain pink with white painted designs.
Height, 70 cm. (27⅝ in.).
Bremen Museum (D. 3724).

8-9 ANCESTOR FIGURE.
Melanesia (Yuat River region, New Guinea).
Heavy, dark wood. Forehead and mouth painted red. Traces of yellow-ochre paint on the face. Mother-of-pearl eyes.
Height, 56.5 cm. (22¼ in.).
Serge Brignoni Collection, Berne.

10 DANCE DRUM.
Melanesia (Sepik River, New Guinea).
Drum in the shape of an hour-glass (a characteristic shape for New Guinea). The tympanum at one end is of skin. The handle is in the form of a human mask surmounted by a hornbill.

Wood, with red and white colouring.
Height, 60 cm. (21⅝ in.).
British Museum, London.

11 DANCE DRUM.
Melanesia (Sepik River, New Guinea).
Plain, dark, heavy wood. The handle is a highly
naturalistic representation of a crocodile.
Height, 58 cm. (22⅞ in.).
Berlin Museum (VI. 41774).

12 POST FROM A MEN'S CEREMONIAL HOUSE.
Melanesia (Island of Siar, Astrolabe Bay, New
Guinea).
Heavy, pale, carved wood.
Height, 210 cm. (82⅝ in.).
Bremen Museum (D. 3063).

13 CARVING FROM A CEREMONIAL HOUSE.
Melanesia (Island of Seleo, North Coast of New
Guinea).
Unpainted brown wood.
Height, 263 cm. (103½ in.).
Berne Museum (D. 4721).

14 CEREMONIAL SHIELD.
Melanesia (Banaro group, Sepik River region, New
Guinea).
Flat wickerwork, oval in shape and bound round the
edge with cassowary feathers. The front is painted with
clay and covered with boars' tusks and cowrie and
nassa shells. The upper half is a head fashioned in clay
on a human skull. The nose is extended into a trunk
with wickerwork, the eyes are of mother-of-pearl, and
the sides have snail shells and boars' tusks added. The
hollow at the back of this and other ceremonial
shields contains miniature tools and weapons, such as
bows and arrows.
Height, 130 cm. (51⅛ in.).
Lateran Museum, Rome (Au. 2262 A.).

15 LARGE RITUAL BOARD IN OPENWORK CARVING.
Melanesia (Sepik Delta, New Guinea).
Boards of this kind of openwork carving were sometimes used for panelling the inside walls of ceremonial
houses. The highly stylised design may be derived
from ancestor figures.
Heavy, dark wood, unpainted.

Height, 185 cm. (72⅞ in.).
Bremen Museum (D. 3505).

16 GABLE DECORATION FOR A CEREMONIAL HOUSE.
Melanesia (Middle Sepik River, New Guinea).
The gables of the meeting houses usually have orna-
ments of this sort, in clay, pot-like knobs, also in clay,
or wooden carvings. The ornaments and carvings
nearly always show the head motif with other human
or bird characteristics.
Clay, burnt partly red, partly black.
Height, 48·5 cm. (19 in.).
Basle Museum (V b. 9355).

17 ANCESTRAL SKULL WITH THE FACE MODELLED IN
CLAY.
Melanesia (Middle Sepik River, New Guinea).
These ancestral skulls are kept in long rows on boards
—often artistically carved—or painted pieces of sago-
palm bark, inside the ceremonial houses.
The flesh is replaced by a coat of clay, and the eyes
with cypraea shells. Tufts of real human hair are
cemented into the skull, and the forehead decoration is
indicated by grey seeds (Job's tears) which have been
pressed into the clay. The face shows the type of decoration, in earth colours, worn on ceremonial occasions.
Bremen Museum (D. 4065).

18 SUSPENSION HOOK.
Melanesia (Lower Sepik River, New Guinea).
See note for plate 2.
Height, 71 cm. (28 in.).
Bremen Museum (D. 4100).

19 SUSPENSION HOOK.
Melanesia (Lower Sepik River, New Guinea).
See note for plate 2.
Height, 85 cm. (33½ in.).
Bremen Museum (D. 4049).

20 DANCE MASK.
Melanesia (Lower Sepik River, New Guinea).
Wood, painted black, white and red; tufts of real
human hair as worn by the inhabitants of the Sepik
area; mother-of-pearl eyes.
Height (without hair), 35 cm. (13¾ in.).
Bremen Museum (D. 3770).

23

21 MASK.
Melanesia (Lower Sepik River, New Guinea).
Flat wickerwork of thin strips of reed, bound with black cassowary feathers round the edge.
Height (without feathers), 35 cm. (13¾ in.).
Berne Museum (Pap. 1135).

22 DANCE HEADDRESS.
Melanesia (Orokolo, southern New Guinea).
Figure in the shape of a bird with human head made of bark cloth over a light frame of reeds. Forehead, nose and mouth painted red; pennon-shaped area round the eyes, black; triangle in front of the ears and section below the mouth, white. Wig made of human hair. Legs made of small wooden pegs which are stuck into wearer's hair.
Height, 40 cm. (15¾ in.); length, 47 cm. (18½ in.).
Serge Brignoni Collection, Berne.

23 FIGURE OF ANCESTOR OR SPIRIT.
Melanesia (Mundugumor group, Yuat River, New Guinea).
Heavy, dark, carved wood. Beard of human hair, nose ornament of boar tusk with two human molars. Ear ornaments: left, a conus-shell ring, right, a nautilus-shell spiral; eyes inlaid with the same irridescent shell. Band of cypraea shell round the forehead; head decoration of human hair with bunch of cassowary feathers.
Height (without feathers), 46 cm. (18⅛ in.).
Serge Brignoni Collection, Berne.

24 FIGURE OF ANCESTOR OR SPIRIT.
Melanesia (south-west Dutch New Guinea).
Light-brown natural wood, hollows in arms and legs rubbed with red. Knotted headdress, bunch of cassowary feathers and seeds (Job's tears) as ear ornaments; grass apron.
Height, 75·5 cm. (29¾ in.).
Basle Museum (V b. 6106).

25 DECORATION FOR PROW OF CANOE.
Melanesia (Dutch New Guinea).
Brown wood, painted black and white with a touch of red.
Height, 85 cm. (33½ in.).
Basle Museum (V b. 6155).

26 KOROWAAR.
Melanesia (Geelvink Bay, Dutch New Guinea).
"Korowaar" ("Korovar" or "Korwar"), is the name given to the ancestor or spirit figures of the Geelvink Bay in north-west New Guinea. Originally, the head of the statue was hollowed out so that a real human skull could be placed inside it.
Plain brown wood, unpainted.
Height, 33 cm. (13 in.).
Frankfurt a.M. Museum.

27 DOUBLE FIGURE.
Melanesia (Trobriand Islands, eastern New Guinea).
Purpose unknown (possibly carved in recent times for trade). Solid, heavy wood; the incised parts have been rubbed with lime.
Height, 50 cm. (19⅝ in.).
Museo Preistorico-etnografico, Rome.

28 CARVING FROM A CEREMONIAL BOARD (called "GOPE" or "KWOI").
Melanesia (Purari Delta, southern New Guinea).
Carved oval boards, pointed at the ends, are put up in the enormous sib long-houses in which the natives of the swampy Purari Delta live (several families share such a house between them, each with a separate compartment; a single long-house thus resembles a terrace of dwellings in an English town). The boards are hung between trophies of skulls, those of humans and of sacrificial pigs, and serve as carriers of supernatural power. The relationship between them and a person is such that a transference of power may occur.
Width, 21 cm. (8¼ in.).
Hamburg Museum (39.24:4).

29 CEREMONIAL ("GOPE") BOARD.
Melanesia (Village of Ukurawi, Purari Delta, southern New Guinea).
See note on plate 28.
Natural coloured, brown wood. Eyes, mouth and surrounding areas and circles filled in in red; the remaining hollows filled in mostly in white.
Height, 102 cm. (40⅛ in.).
Basle Museum (V b. 7847).

30 FIGURE OF ANCESTOR OR SPIRIT.
Melanesia (Lake Sentania, Dutch New Guinea).
A rare double figure, possibly representing mother and

child. The statue stood in the hut of the chieftain of Ifar, in Lake Sentania.
Heavy, natural coloured, pale brown wood.
Height, 85 cm. (33½ in.).
Basle Museum (V b. 6659).

31 POST FROM A MEN'S CEREMONIAL (CLUB) HOUSE.
Melanesia (Tami Islands, Huon Gulf, New Guinea).
These figures, carved of heavy, dark wood, and representing chiefs, serve as corner posts to support the raised floor of the men's ceremonial houses.
Height, 175 cm. (68⅞ in.).
Hamburg Museum (1665[1]).

32 CARVED BOARD FROM PROW OF CANOE.
Melanesia (Trobriand Islands, eastern New Guinea).
Carvings such as this are fitted to the prow of the large trading canoes of the natives of Kiriwina Island.
Brown wood, painted white and red.
Height, 57 cm. (22½ in.).
Museo Preistorico-etnografico, Rome.

33 SHIELD.
Melanesia (Papuan Gulf, southern New Guinea).
The shield is carried in a sling of bark cloth across the archer's left shoulder so that the upper arm rests in the rectangular cut-out space. Nothing is known about the meaning of the two-headed figure.
Wooden board, painted red (mainly the figure and the rectangular surround) and white.
Height, 95 cm. (37⅜ in.).
Völkerkundliche Sammlung, Burgdorf (Switzerland).

34 DANCE MASK IN THE FORM OF A FISH.
Melanesia (Mabuiag Island, Torres Straits).
Made of pieces of turtle shell tied together; engraved parts rubbed with lime; mother-of-pearl eyes. Decorated with cassowary feathers.
Length, 127 cm. (50 in.).
British Museum, London.

35 DANCE MASK.
Melanesia (Torres Straits Islands).
Composed of small, partly bent, pieces of turtle shell. Ear ornaments of small haliotis shells.
Height, 55 cm. (21⅝ in.).
Berlin Museum (VI. 653).

36 LARGE RITUAL FIGURE.
Melanesia (Middle Sepik River, New Guinea).
These statues stand by the artificial earth mounds, which are fenced in and planted with ornamental shrubs, in front of the large, imposing ceremonial houses.
Very heavy, dark wood. Face painted white and black, with mouth only in pink; rest of body black and white with a touch of pink.
Height, 201 cm. (79⅛ in.).
Serge Brignoni Collection, Berne.

37 FUNERAL FIGURE.
Melanesia (Village of Panakondo, New Ireland).
Such figures, called "Uli" and sometimes representing ancestors, are exhibited in special huts during funeral ceremonies (women are forbidden to attend these ceremonies which may go on for several years). Unlike the Málanggan carvings (see plates 38, 39, 40, 42) Uli figures are not destroyed after the ceremony but wrapped up and kept in the ceremonial houses. The apparent dual sexuality is not intended to be realistic; it should perhaps be interpreted as a symbol of fertility.
Heavy brown wood, with traces of white and red colour.
Height, 160 cm. (63 in.).
Hamburg Museum (502[1]).

38 FUNERAL CARVING.
Melanesia (New Ireland).
Carvings of this type, known as Málanggan, are specially made for funeral ceremonies. The New Ireland natives are divided into two social groups or moieties, and husband and wife must always belong to opposite divisions. When a person dies, the Málanggan carvings for the funeral are always carved by members of the other social group, not by those of his own. Different ancestral lineages have the proprietary rights to their own designs. Nothing definite is known about the significance of the devouring motif which occurs frequently. Possibly the idea underlying the carving is based on the astral myth according to which the frog of the bright moon swallows the wife of the dark moon.
Wood, painted white and red. The eyes of both figures are made of green turbo shell opercula.
Height, 55 cm. (21⅝ in.).
Hamburg Museum (E. 1538).

39. FUNERAL CARVING (MÁLANGGAN).
Melanesia (New Ireland).
See note for plate 38.
Hornbill on top of a serpent; another serpent between the head, wings and tail of the bird. Underneath the beak a small man is sitting on the serpent holding a black, round object, perhaps a taro root, in his hands. Light, pale wood, painted black, white and red. Eyes made of green turbo shell opercula.
Height, 32 cm. (12⅝ in.); width 66 cm. (26 in.).
Hamburg Museum (E. 1535).

40 FUNERAL CARVING (MÁLANGGAN).
Melanesia (New Ireland).
See note for plate 38.
This cockatoo or cock forms the prow figure of a ritual boat which also contains a large figure of an ancestor. Light wood, covered with lime; the bird's comb as well as the head and leg ornaments painted red.
Height, 39 cm. (15⅜ in.).
Hamburg Museum (2613:05).

41 DANCE MASK.
Melanesia (New Ireland).
Section of a face in wood, painted black, white and red. Eyes made of green turbo shell opercula. Plaited grass rings as ear ornaments. Hat and head wrapping of brown bark cloth.
Height, 26 cm. (10¼ in.).
Hamburg Museum (E. 437).

42 FUNERAL CARVING (MÁLANGGAN).
Melanesia (New Ireland).
See note for plate 38.
During funeral ceremonies these friezes, together with Uli and other carvings, are exhibited in special huts standing in a fenced-in area.
Frieze of light, pale wood, carved in the shape of a bird (hawk) holding a serpent in its beak and between its feet. Two more small birds are resting on the stylised wings. Painted black, white and red (as are most Málanggan figures).
Length, 107 cm. (42⅛ in.).
Hamburg Museum (E. 1537).

43 FIGURE WITH OUTSTRETCHED ARMS.
Melanesia (New Ireland).
This statue, carved in the style of the Uli (*see note for plate 37*), shows a male figure encircled by a serpent and standing in an open tridacna shell.
Wood, painted black, white and red.
Height, 115 cm. (45¼ in.).
Hamburg Museum (E. 2448).

44 DANCE MASK.
Melanesia (Duke of York Islands).
Cane wicker frame covered with strips of bark fibre; face of bark fibre covered with lime; eyes, nose and mouth painted black. Mother-of-pearl eyes with pupils of dark polydonta opercula. Conical wooden sticks as decoration at the side of the nose and as teeth inside the mouth.
Height, 38 cm. (15 in.).
Hamburg Museum (17.74:108).

45 DANCE MASK.
Melanesia (Duke of York Islands).
Section of a face in pale wood, painted white and red. Beard of fibre, head covering of grass.
Height, 34 cm. (13⅜ in.).
Hamburg Museum (E. 1479).

46 DANCE MASK.
Melanesia (Sulka group, New Britain).
Cane frame covered with pith pads dyed red; head, neck section and hands in wood. Red, with some white and green colour. Grass skirt.
Height (without skirt), 80 cm. (31½ in.).
Hamburg Museum (12.135:256).

47 DANCE MASK.
Melanesia (Sulka group, New Britain).
As plate 46, but with wooden ears; hat decorated with grass instead of cassowary feathers.
Height (without grass skirt), 72 cm. (28⅜ in.).
Bremen Museum (D. 3057).

48 DANCE MASK.
Melanesia (Baining group, Gazelle Peninsula, New Britain).
The masked dances of the Bainings, the oldest, pre-Austronesian inhabitants of the island, are primarily directed towards increasing the fertility of fields and game animals and spirits.
Natural coloured, light fig-tree bark over a frame of thin, bent sticks; painted black and reddish-yellow.

Height, 100 cm. (39¾ in.).
Hamburg Museum (1188:33).

49 DANCE MASK.
Melanesia (Baining group, Gazelle Peninsula, New Britain).
See note for plate 48.
Height, 82 cm. (32¼ in.).
Hamburg Museum.

50 DANCE MASK.
Melanesia (Sulka group, New Britain).
Head in wood, carved in the round. Parts painted in red, white and black. Head decoration of black cassowary feathers. The mask is carried on the head in such a way that the bunch of leaves hides the face.
Height (without leaves), 42 cm. (16½ in.).
Hamburg Museum (14.91:8).

51 DANCE MASK.
Melanesia (Sulka group, New Britain).
A light frame of supple sticks is covered with pith pads, dyed red. These are stitched on and painted all over with green, black and white ornaments. The head and edge of this wing-shaped structure are covered with cassowary feathers. A garment of leaves conceals the body of the wearer.
Height, 120 cm. (47¼ in.).
Bremen Museum.

52 FOOD BOWL IN THE FORM OF A PIG.
Melanesia (San Cristoval, Solomon Islands).
Carved from a piece of wood dyed black, with inlaid, triangular polished pieces of nautilus shell; the eyes are of two cowrie shells.
Length, 49 cm. (19¼ in.); height, 20 cm. (7⅞ in.).
Basle Museum (V. 7182).

53 FOOD BOWL.
Melanesia (Solomon Islands).
Thin wood, stained black. Eyes inlaid with nautilus shell. The cross-section of the bowl is oval.
Height, 17 cm. (6¾ in.).
Josef Müller Collection, Solothurn.

54 TRIDACNA CARVING.
Melanesia (Choiseul, Solomon Islands).

These carvings, produced by the lengthy and extremely difficult process of sawing the giant tridacna shell with rattan cane, sand and water, serve to close the gable-ends of the miniature huts in which the skulls of dead chiefs are preserved.
Height, 23·5 cm. (9¼ in.); width 30·5 cm. (12 in.); depth, 3 cm. (1⅛ in.).
Basle Museum (V b. 7731).

55 TRIDACNA CARVING.
Melanesia (Choiseul, Solomon Islands).
See note for plate 54.
Height, 30·8 cm. (12 in.); width 13 cm. (5⅛ in.).
Basle Museum (V. 7517).

56 CANOE PROW FIGURE.
Melanesia (Maravo Lagoon, New Georgia, Solomon Islands).
The figure is fixed to the bows of the war canoe, just above water-level, where the line of the keel meets the tall, vertical prow. It is supposed to represent a good spirit who is to protect the boat against misfortune. The ear ornaments worn by the local inhabitants are faithfully rendered in the form of a wooden ring fitted into a hole in the lobe.
Wood, dyed black, eyes and z-shaped decorative lines in the face are of nautilus mother-of-pearl.
Height, 17 cm. (6¾ in.).
Basle Museum (V b. 7525).

57 STONE FIGURE.
Melanesia (Choiseul, Solomon Islands).
Age, significance and use unknown.
Grey, porous stone.
Height, 48·5 cm. (19 in.).
Basle Museum (V b. 7495).

58 DANCE SHIELD.
Melanesia (Solomon Islands).
The front of this extremely beautifully and carefully plaited cane shield has been painted over with a gum mixture and coloured red and black. This surface has been inlaid with a figure mosaic made up of countless square-ground plates of nautilus shell.
Height, 91 cm. (35⅞ in.).
Cambridge Museum.

59 MASK.
Melanesia (Nissan, Solomon Islands).
These masks are worn by the men of a secret society and represent a spirit called "Kokorra".
Hat and face section of palm fronds painted white and black; ears of pieces of wood. With the mask goes a poncho-like garment of beaten bark.
Height, 74 cm. (29⅛ in.).
Bremen Museum (D. 6319).

60 STATUE
Melanesia (Island of Vanua Lava, Banks Islands).
Such statues are put up in front of houses or in the jungle in honour of the dead. The number of heads is intended to show that their owner had the magic power or "Mana" of several men; it is also indicative of his rank within the graded society known as Suque.
Carved from black tree-fern pith.
Height, 180 cm. (70⅞ in.).
Basle Museum (V b. 4450).

61 STATUE.
Melanesia (Gaua, Banks Islands).
See note for plate 60.
Carved from black tree-fern pith.
Height, 187 cm. (73⅝ in.).
Basle Museum (V b. 4374).

62 MASK OF A SECRET SOCIETY (TAMATE).
Melanesia (Ambrym, New Hebrides).
The conical headdress is made of wood fibre over a frame of sticks; banana fibre, representing beard and hair, forms a fringe. On top the sticks are inserted into a piece of banana skin with a bunch of feathers tied to the top. The face is painted red and green. A garment of leaves which envelops the rest of the body is worn with the mask.
Height (without beard), 68 cm. (26¾ in.).
Hamburg Museum (E. 1033).

63 DANCE MASK.
Melanesia (Purari Delta, southern New Guinea).
Bark cloth painted black, white and red, stretched over a frame of thin sticks. Blades of grass have been stitched on to outline the different areas of colour.
Height, 79 cm. (31⅛ in.).
Hamburg Museum.

64 STATUE.
Melanesia (Banks Islands).
The significance of such dancing figures is unknown. The figure consists of a frame of thin sticks covered with palm sheaths; black and dark-red ornaments have been painted on a white ground.
Height, 94 cm. (37 in.).
Hamburg Museum (22:08).

65 TREE-FERN STATUE.
Melanesia (south-east Ambrym, New Hebrides).
Statue of a male secret society.
Carved from black tree-fern pith.
Height, 163 cm. (64⅛ in.).
Hamburg Museum (14.136:318).

66 DANCE MASK.
Melanesia (New Caledonia).
The mask is used in mimes and is intended to represent a water demon.
Face section of wood, painted black; pad of hair and beard consisting of tufts of human hair; feather covering made of net with black and dark reddish-brown Notu pigeon feathers knotted into the meshes.
Paris, Musée de l'Homme (80-39-4).

67 SPIRIT FIGURE.
Melanesia (New Caledonia).
Such figures served to give protection for magical purposes, such as rain-making.
Hard wood, dyed black.
Height, 37·5 cm. (14¾ in.).
Basle Museum (V b. 1401).

68 ANCESTOR FIGURE.
Melanesia (Admiralty Islands).
Light wood, painted red, incised parts filled in with lime. The custom of piercing and elongating the ear lobes, widespread in Melanesia, is clearly indicated.
Height, 54 cm. (21¼ in.).
Bremen Museum (D. 8141).

69 ANCESTOR FIGURE.
Melanesia (Admiralty Islands).
Brown wood, painted light-red and white.
Height, 173 cm. (68⅛ in.).
Bremen Museum (D. 10787).

70 SACRED STATUE.

Micronesia (Nukuoro, Central Caroline Islands).

Representation of the god Sope.

The Micronesian Island of Nukuoro was settled by a reverse migration of Polynesians from the east. This perhaps accounts for the existence of statues of mythical deities who were worshipped by the priests in the temples. (Collected by J. St. Kubary in 1877.)

Coarse fibred, reddish-brown wood.

Height, 168 cm. (66¼ in.).

Hamburg Museum (E. 1893).

71 MASK.

Micronesia (Island of Satoan, Mortlock Group, Central Caroline Islands).

The Mortlock Islands are the only Micronesian archipelago where masks are worn. This mask depicts a sacred, good spirit. The dances at which it is worn are performed on the beach to ward off the danger of typhoons and they probably have as a secondary object the promotion of the bread-fruit harvest.

Pale wood, covered with white chalk and black paint in front.

Height, 112 cm. (44⅛ in.).

Hamburg Museum (He. 4382).

72 STATUE.

Melanesia (Island of Kaniet).

Figure carvings are extremely rare on the Island of Kaniet. Nothing is known about the significance and use of this statue.

Carved of light-brown, hard wood; the feet may have been cut off.

Height, 81 cm. (31⅞ in.).

Bremen Museum (D. 2190).

73 HEI-TIKI.

Polynesia (New Zealand).

Such ornaments were worn as neck pendants. The hands have three fingers only, indicating that the figure represented was a supernatural being. Tiki is the Polynesian name for the demi-god who created the first human being; later it became the Polynesian description for images of deities generally. (Hei-Tiki means neck-Tiki.)

The material is nephrite, a hard green stone (also used for tools and weapons) found only in one small area of the South Island of New Zealand. The eye sockets are inlaid with serrated rings of haliotis shell.

Height, 19·5 cm. (7¾ in.).

Josef Müller Collection, Solothurn.

74 PART OF A FRIEZE FROM A TRIBAL MEETING HOUSE.

Polynesia (New Zealand).

The carving from the front gable shows the so-called "manaia" motif, an ancestor figure flanked on either side by a mythical creature, a demon with the head of a bird.

Plain wood, painted red. The eye motifs of the upper border are of iridescent green haliotis shell pieces.

Height, 55 cm. (21⅝ in.).

Hamburg Museum.

75 WALL PANEL FROM A TRIBAL MEETING HOUSE.

Polynesia (New Zealand).

The interior walls of this house are made of wooden boards with figure carving, alternating with screens made of wooden rods or reeds painted red, white and black and tied together in a large variety of designs. This carving alludes to the well-known Polynesian myth according to which the demi-god Maui is supposed to have fished certain islands—referred to as fishes —out of the sea. The Maori name for the North Island of New Zealand, "te ika a Maui" (fish of Maui) is a reference to this myth. The carving of the face shows the characteristic Maori tattoo marks in a most naturalistic way. The eyes are composed of pieces of iridescent haliotis shell.

Brownish-black wood.

Height, 215 cm (84⅝ in.).

Hamburg Museum.

76 FIGURE OF AN ANCESTOR.

Polynesia (New Zealand).

Possibly a figure from the prow carving of a war canoe. The carving is so fixed that the face looks into the vessel.

Firm wood; very old work.

Height, 66 cm. (26 in.).

British Museum, London (1904-245).

77 PROW OF A WAR CANOE.

Polynesia (New Zealand).

The sea-going war canoes of the Maori are distinguished

by their rich carvings, especially at the prow. Besides figures they frequently show the spiral patterns which are typical of Maori art, carried out in beautiful open-work carving.
Hard wood, painted a plain dark red.
Length, 127 cm. (50 in.); height, 64·5 cm. (25½ in.).
Hamburg Museum (E. 1798).

78 FIGURE OF A GOD.
Polynesia (Cook Islands).
According to the only evidence from an old source, that of the missionary Williams (1839), the subject represented is the god of fishermen. Fishing canoes carried these images on their prows; the natives sacrificed to them before expeditions and prayed to them for success.
Height, 44 cm. (17⅜ in.).
British Museum, London (London Missionary Soc.).

79 STATUE OF A GOD.
Polynesia (Cook Islands).
See note for plate 78.
The figure is painted with the tattoo motifs formerly found on the Cook Islands, although the marks are not always on the right parts of the body.
Height, 31·5 cm. (12½ in.).
British Museum, London (9866).

80–81 FIGURE OF A GOD.
Polynesia (Rarotonga, Cook Islands).
It is doubtful whether this statue is correctly described as "The god Te Rongo with his three sons" (Rongo was the god of cultivation).
A unique example.
Height, 69 cm. (27⅛ in.).
British Museum, London (London Missionary Soc.).

82 FIGURE OF A GOD.
Polynesia (Rurutu, Tubuai Islands).
The figure represents the Polynesian god of the Ocean, Tangaroa, at the moment of the creation of other gods and human beings. The hollow figure closed at the back with a lid which also has small figure carvings, contains a few loose figures inside.
A unique example.
Pale, hard wood.
Height, 112 cm. (44⅛ in.).
British Museum, London.

83 TEMPLE FIGURE.
Polynesia (Kailua, Hawaii).
Probably representing the god of War, Ku.
These wooden statues stood in the temple enclosures ("heiau") in which the high priests lived.
Height, 77 cm. (30¼ in.).
British Museum, London.

84 HEAD OF A GOD.
Polynesia (Hawaii).
Image of the old Hawaiian god of War, Kukailimoku.
A narrow-meshed net is drawn over a wickerwork base. Into this are knotted innumerable tiny yellow and red feathers of the Mamo, Oo (yellow) and Iiwi (red) birds. The eyes are of mother-of-pearl with black wooden buttons as pupils; the head is adorned with human hair. The mouth contains filed dog's teeth.
The figure was presented to Göttingen in 1781–2, together with other Polynesian ethnographical specimens from Captain Cook's third voyage.
Height, 47 cm. (18½ in.).
Göttingen Museum.

85 HEAD OF A GOD.
Polynesia (Hawaii).
See note for plate 84.
Height, 55 cm. (21⅝ in.).
Berlin Museum (VI. 253).

86 BOWL.
Polynesia (Hawaii).
Hard, brown wood; mother-of-pearl eyes; pieces of bone as teeth. The perforations in the figures suggest that this bowl was intended for liquids.
Height, 25 cm. (9⅞ in.); length, 48 cm. (18⅞ in.).
British Museum, London.

87 BOWL.
Polynesia (Hawaii).
Carved of hard, brown wood.
Height, 19 cm. (7½ in.).
British Museum, London.

88 FIGURE OF A GOD OR GODDESS.
Polynesia (Hawaii).
Probably this depicts the goddess of volcanoes, Pele.
The figure originally stood in the royal sacred enclosure at Karakakua, Hawaii. From there Midshipman

30

John Knowles of H.M.S. *Blonde* brought it to England in 1825.
Heavy, black wood. Human hair, mother-of-pearl eyes (of which one is missing) with a black button as pupil.
Height, 42 cm. (16½ in.).
British Museum, London.

89 FIGURE OF A GOD OR GODDESS.
Polynesia (Hawaii).
In the year 1819 the Hawaiian king Liholiho or Kamahameha II embarked on a series of revolutionary moves, especially regarding religion. Among these were the abolition of priestly rule, the lifting of the taboo, and the destruction of temples and images of gods. The priests and other native believers, however, hid many of the images in caves and other secret places, and a number have thus been preserved. The present figure, together with other cult objects, was discovered in the year 1880 on a barely accessible rocky shore at Hamakua (Hawaii). According to certain informed natives the figure represents the goddess Kihe wahine (also known as Kiha wahine or Kiha nui lulu moku), goddess of goblins and lizards. It has been carved from the hard brown wood of the Kou tree and is shown in a kneeling position which is otherwise unknown. The mouth has been inset with human teeth; the eyes were originally of mother-of-pearl of which only one disk was left at the time of discovery.
Height, 43 cm. (16⅞ in.).
Berlin Museum (VI. 8375).

90 FIGURE OF A GOD.
Polynesia (Tahiti).
Height, 43 cm. (16⅞ in.).
British Museum, London (7047).

91 TIKI.
Polynesia (Marquesas Islands).
See note for plate 73.
This figure shows something of the unusually artistic tattoo marks with which the Marquesans covered their entire bodies.

Carved from hard, brown wood.
Height, 48 cm. (18⅞ in.).
Cologne Museum (24782).

92 TIKI.
Polynesia (Marquesas Islands).
See note for plate 73.
Grey basalt.
Height, 15 cm. (5⅞ in.).
Paris, Musée de l'Homme (87-50-1).

93 STONE FIGURE.
Polynesia (Necker Island, Hawaii).
Probably an image of a god. The figure was found in 1894, together with a few others, in a sacred enclosure on the island. This tiny island, lying isolated to the north-west of Hawaii, was not inhabited when Europeans discovered it in 1786.
Grey, porous basalt.
Height, 29 cm. (11⅜ in.).
British Museum, London.

94-95 ANCESTOR FIGURE
Polynesia (Easter Island).
Male "skeleton". Ancestor figures of this sort were wrapped in bark cloth and kept inside the houses. At certain religious feasts the people held them in their arms while singing and dancing.
Carved from the reddish-brown, very hard wood of the Toromiro tree. The rims of the eyes are made from hollow sections of bird bone; the pupils are fragments of obsidian.
Height, 44 cm. (17⅜ in.).
British Museum, London.

96 ANCESTOR FIGURE.
Polynesia (Easter Island).
Female ancestor figure of Toromiro wood.
See note for plate 94-95.
Height, 41 cm. (16⅛ in.).
Josef Müller Collection, Solothurn.

PHOTOGRAPHIC SOURCES

Basle: Museum für Völkerkunde

Berlin: Museum für Völkerkunde

Berne: Historisches Museum

Berne: Serge Brignoni Collection

Bremen: Museum für Natur-, Völker- und Handelskunde

Burgdorf (Switzerland): Völkerkundliche Sammlung

Cambridge: Museum of Archaeology and Ethnology

Frankfurt a.M.: Museum für Völkerkunde

Göttingen: Museum für Völkerkunde. University Collection

Hamburg: Museum für Völkerkunde und Vorgeschichte

Cologne: Rautenstrauch-Joest-Museum

London: British Museum

Neuchâtel: Musée ethnographique

Paris: Musée de l'Homme

Rome: Museo Preistorico-etnografico "Luigi Pigorini"

Rome: Museo Missionario-etnografico al Laterano

Solothurn: Josef Müller Collection

The Curators of the Museums and owners of the private collections mentioned above placed their treasures freely at our disposal and showed themselves most anxious to co-operate in every way. It is our pleasant duty to thank them all for their understanding attitude and valuable assistance, which contributed in large measure to the successful outcome of this undertaking.

That these modest acknowledgments omit the names of many another Museum, particularly in Sweden, Denmark and the Netherlands, upon whose funds of unique specimens of Oceanic art we should gladly have drawn, is due mainly to the necessity of confining this book to reasonable proportions and to the other purely practical considerations.

2

4

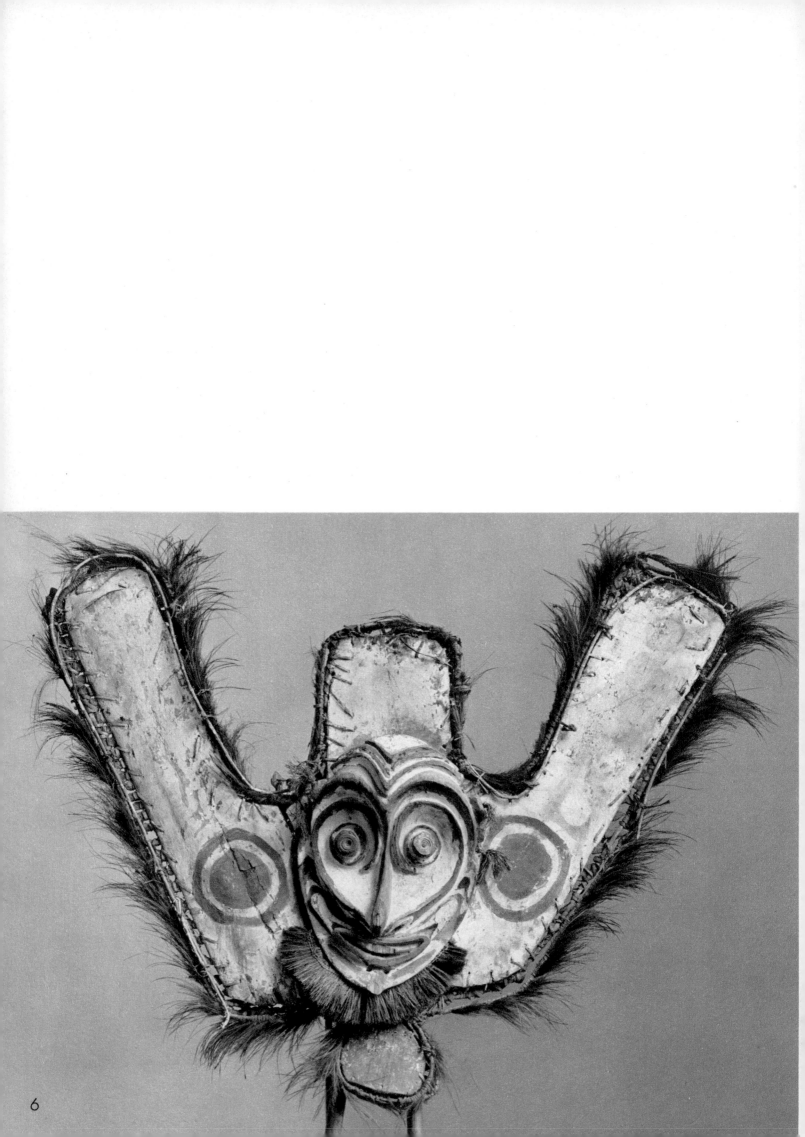

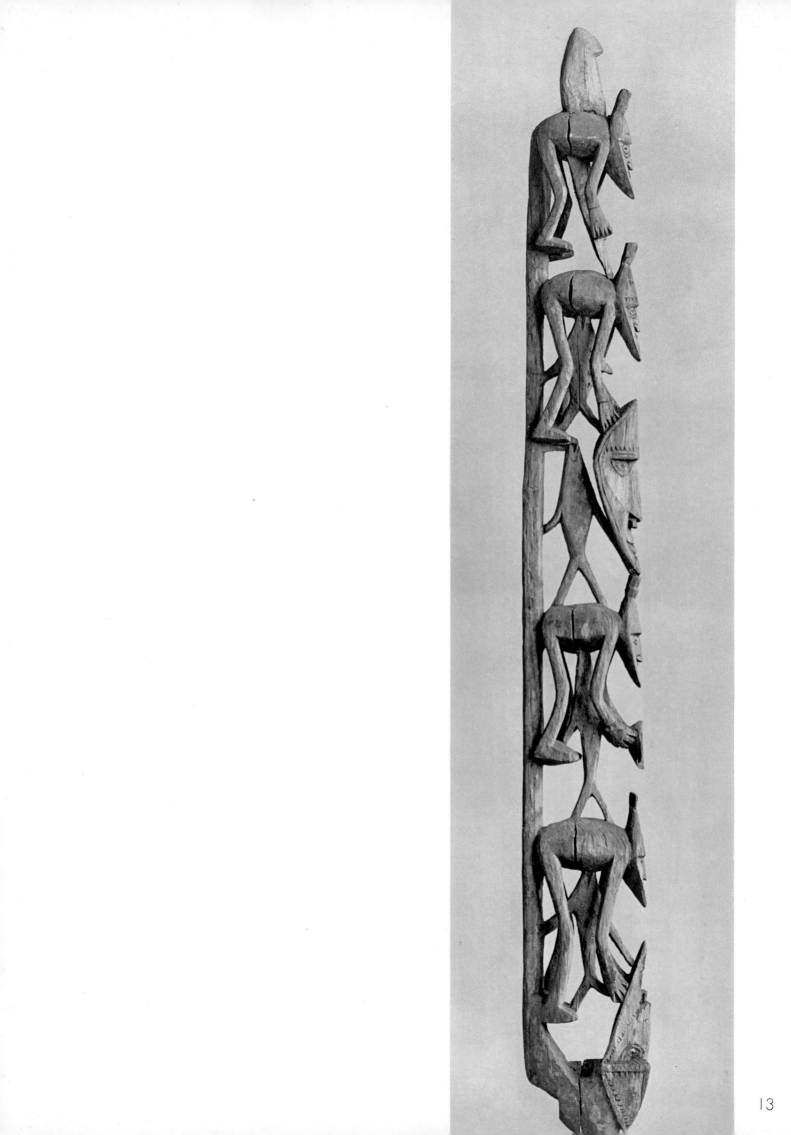

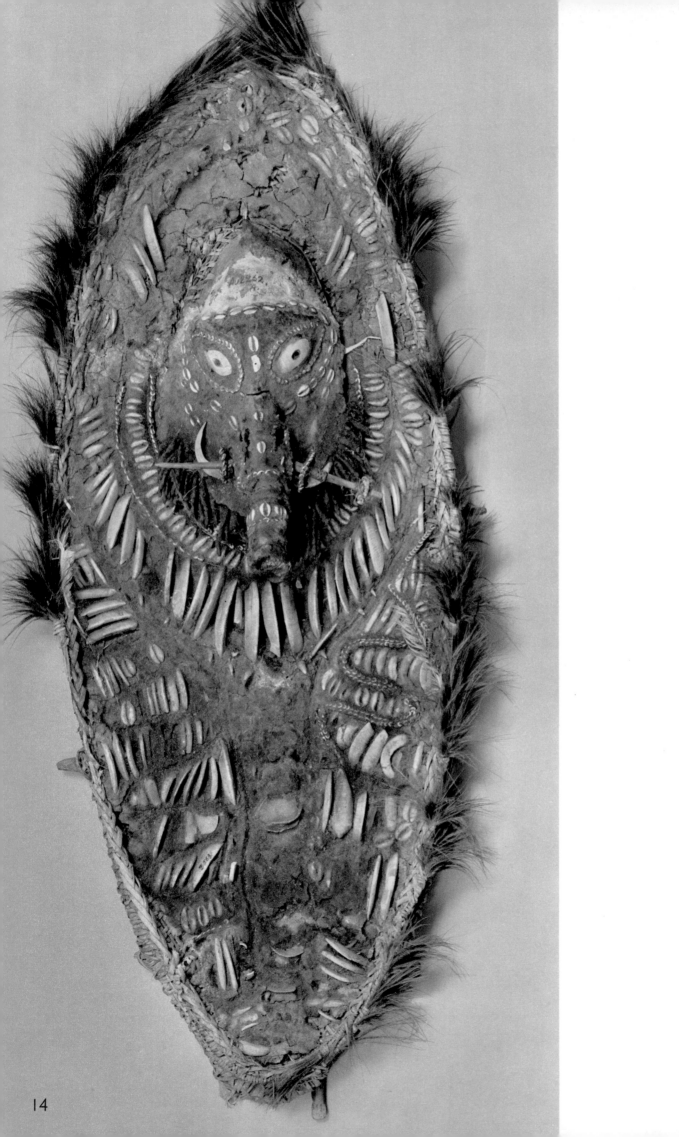

15

16

18

23

24

33

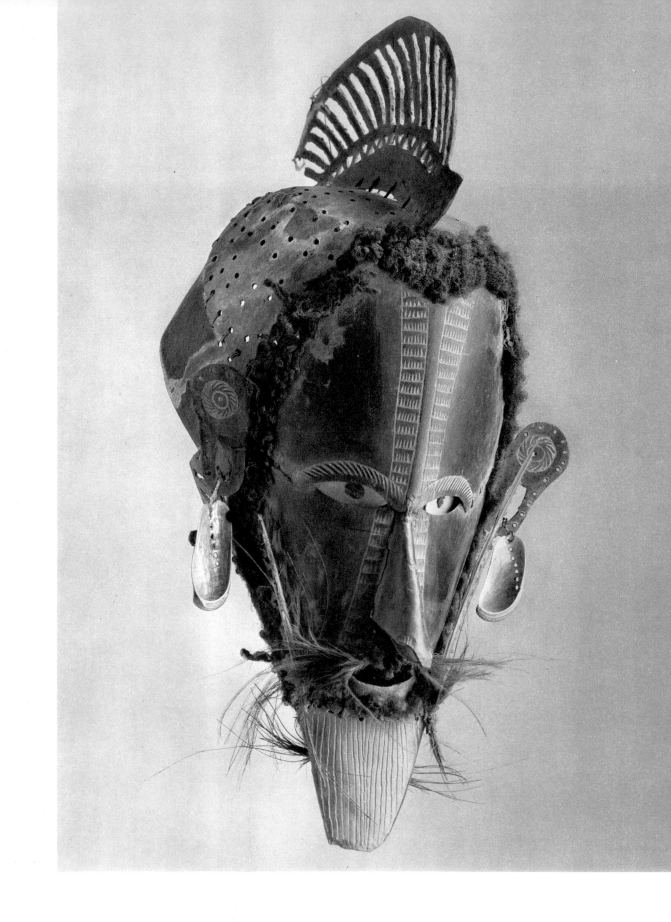

41

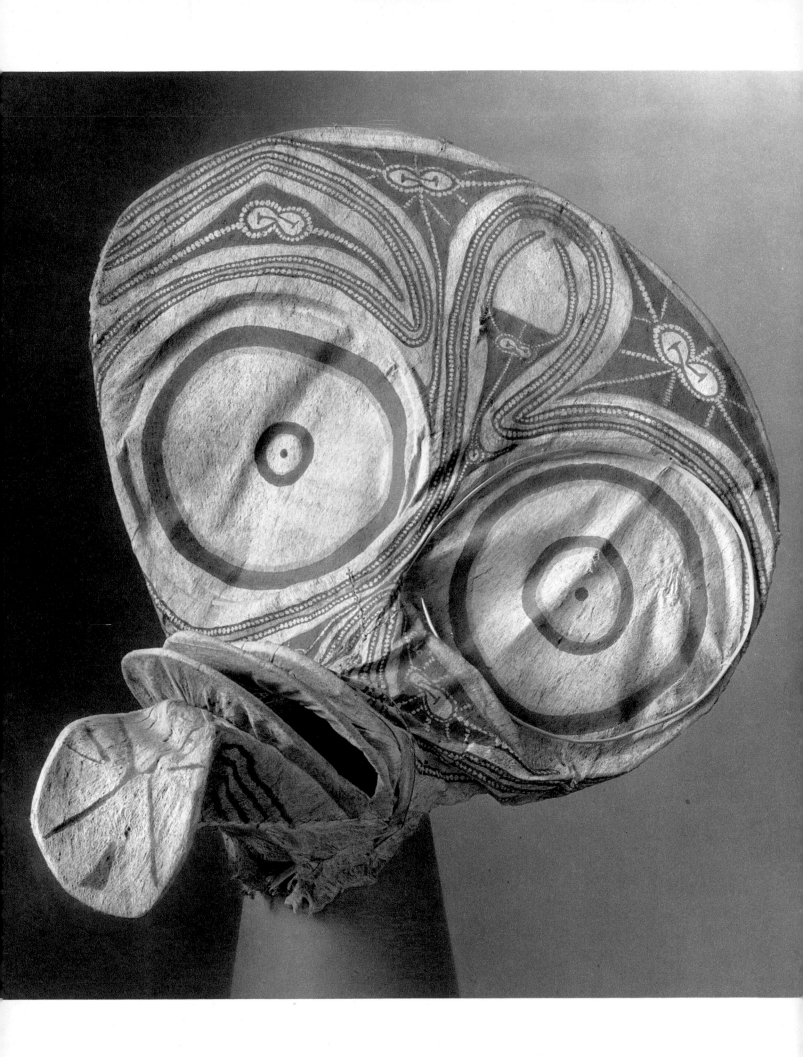

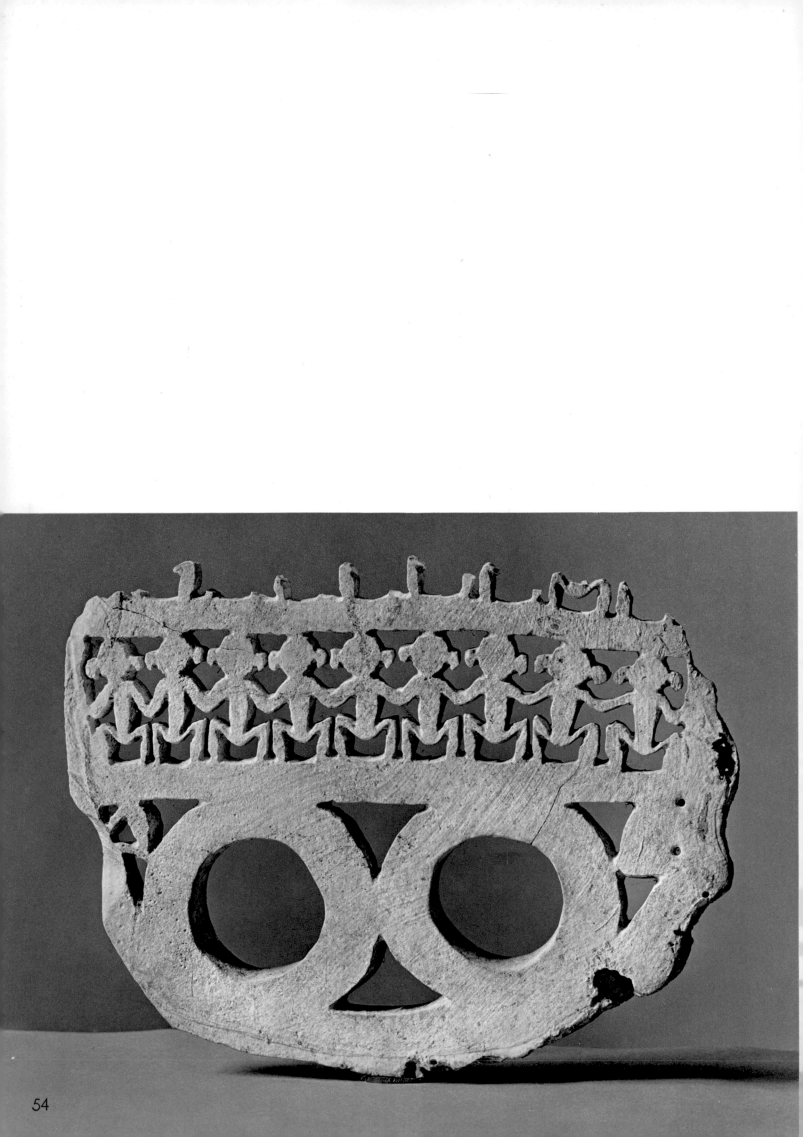

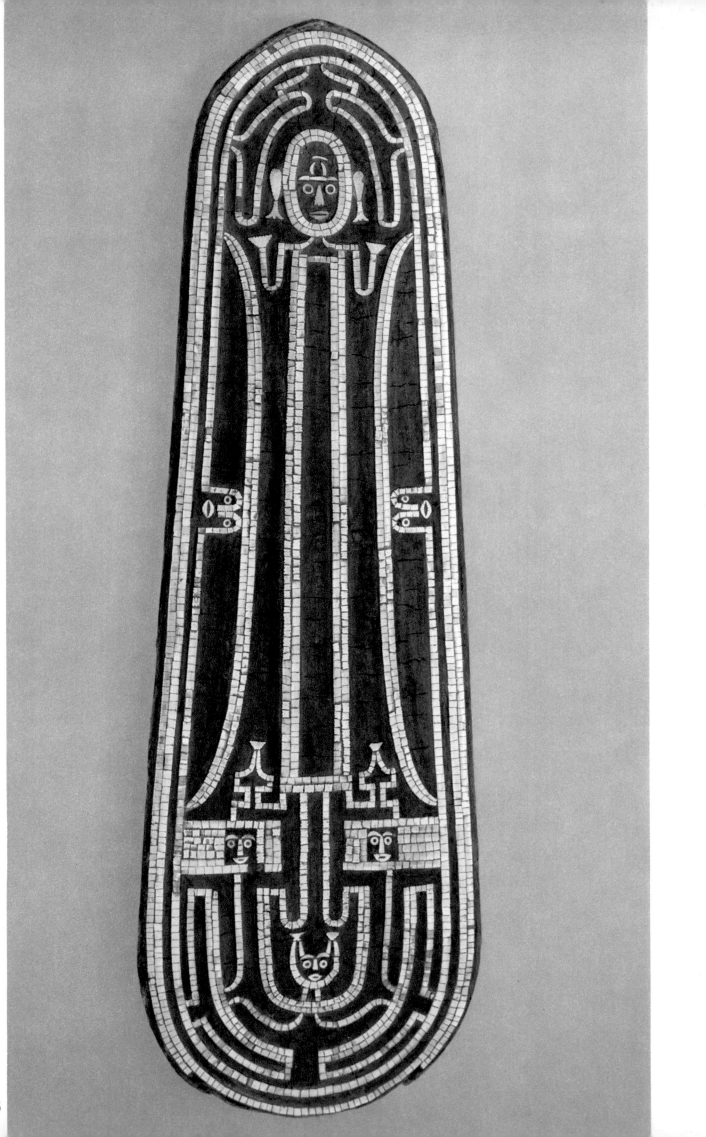

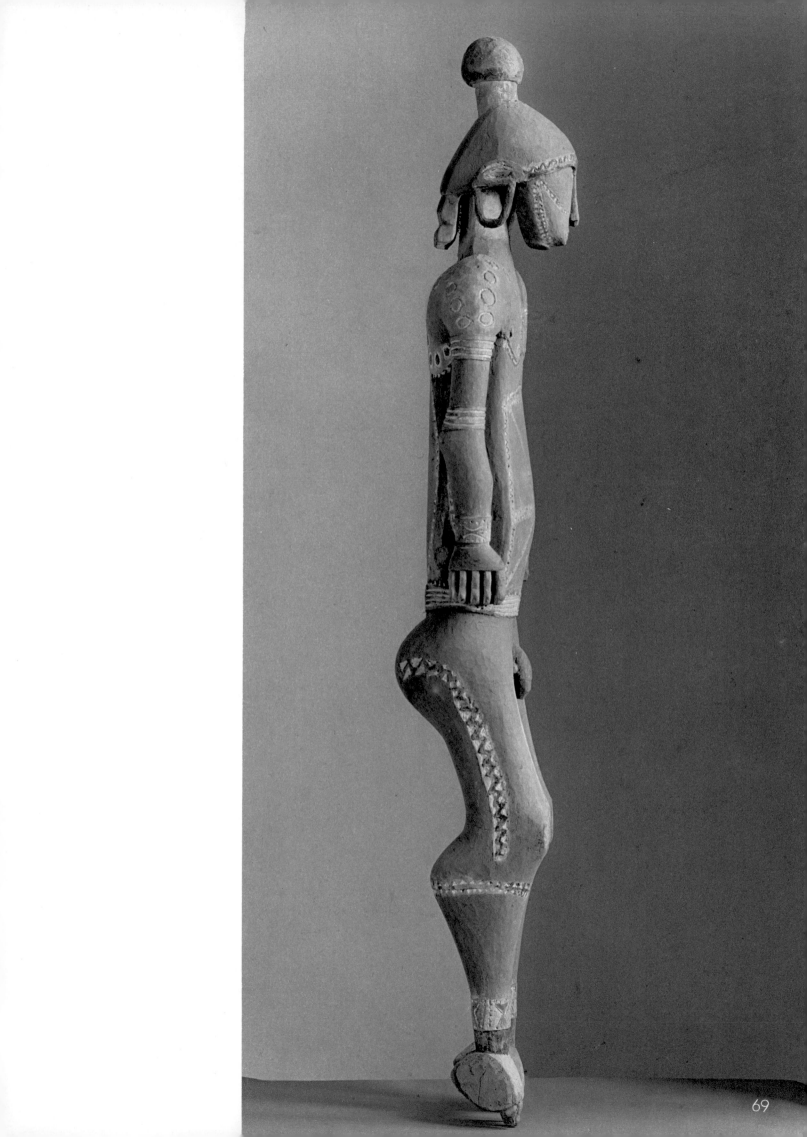

83

94

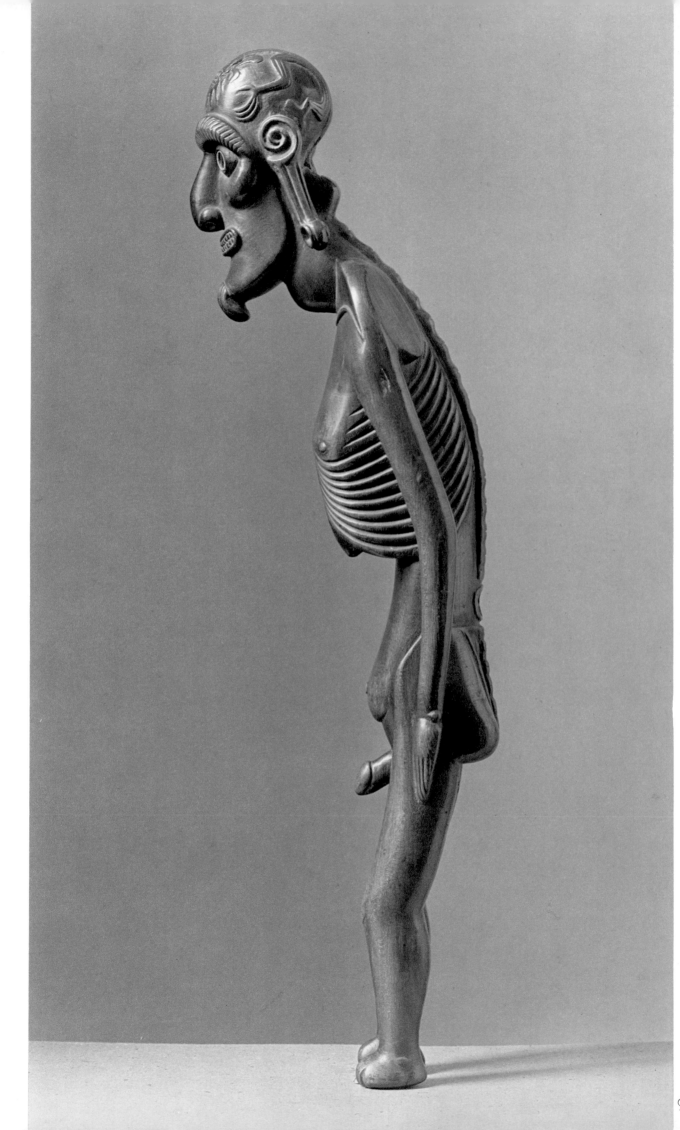

96

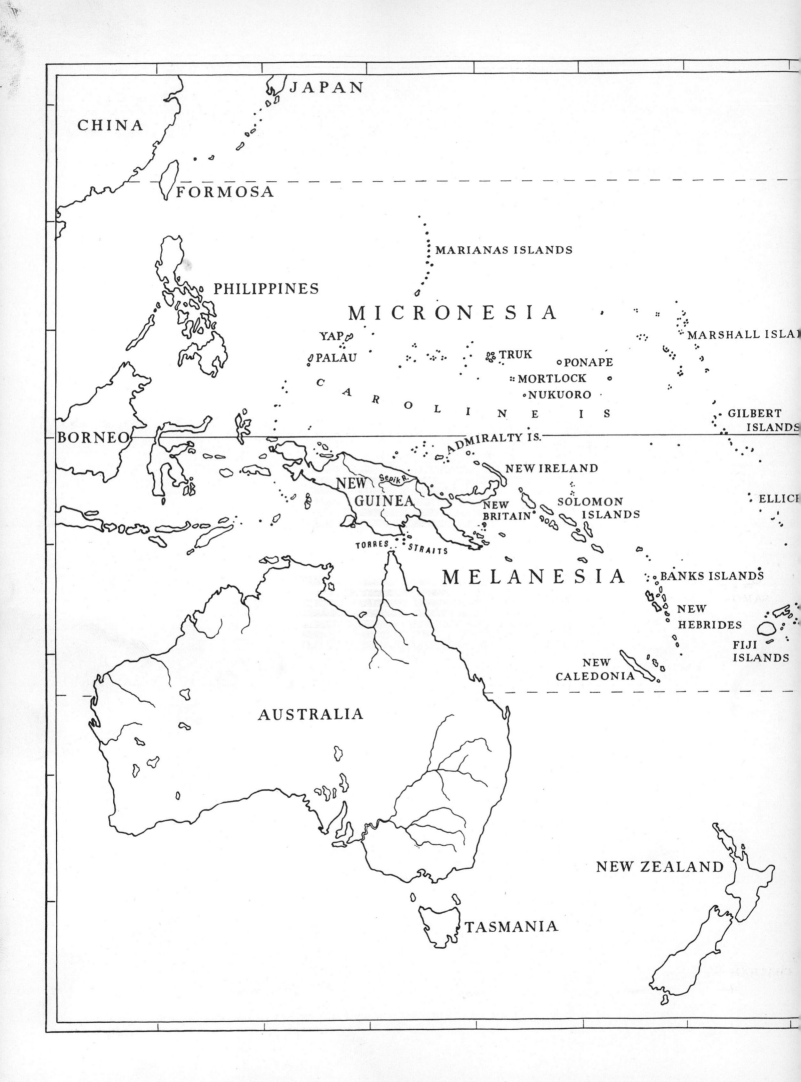